ADVANCE PRAISE

"Eric's book, *Hacking SaaS: An Insider's Guide to Managing Software Business Success*, is a terrific and much-needed explanation of the fundamental business and financial principles of running a SaaS business. Eric bridges the ongoing confusion between well-known financial principles and poorly understood operational metrics that are the basis of the SaaS business model. He approaches the subject with a neutral perspective and an explanation of the basic SaaS structures and tracking mechanisms. He isn't an investor or a SaaS consultant with an eye to hype, nor is he an entrepreneur promoting the value of their way of doing business. Eric's an experienced CFO who has brought order to numerous SaaS companies, helping management and boards get on the same page in terms of what the key management metrics should be, how they are defined, and what they mean."

—**Lauren Kelley, Founder and CEO of OPEXEngine**

"I've known Eric for over fifteen years and have followed his SaaS career through his many thoughtful articles on the subject. It was only natural that when I needed a SaaS business case study for the management team at Key Factor, I turned to Eric. His work provided the team with detailed reviews of Enterprise SaaS companies and helped provoke meaningful discussion. His book, *Hacking SaaS: An Insider's Guide to Managing Software Business Success*, expands the subject far beyond the work he did for us. I'm confident you will find it just as insightful."

—**Jim DeBlasio, CFO and EVP of Operations at KeyFactor**

"Working in the software and tech space for more than twenty years and personally experiencing on-premise perpetual to cloud-based SAAS software transitions, I can attest to the challenges of adopting and managing within this business model. *Hacking SaaS: An Insider's Guide to Managing Software Business Success*, is a must-have resource for the SAAS professional. Eric provides a history of this transition and an in-depth study of the SaaS business model and then connects these details to management and strategy development. He defines every SaaS metric in use today, explains how they are calculated, and describes how they should be used to guide operations and strategy. His book is an invaluable addition to the SaaS industry's knowledge base."

—Ron Fior, Partner at FLG

"As I was promoted to CEO of Swrve to lead its restructuring, Eric was the confident, seasoned, and ingenious right-hand who steered me right from the start. Eric worked with me every step of the way to implement SaaS best practices into our operations—providing data-driven strategic guidance and financial acuity. In his book, *Hacking SaaS: An Insider's Guide to Managing Software Business Success*, Eric consolidates his deep SaaS experience into a resource that SaaS professionals can rely upon, just as I did during my CEO tenure."

—Lisa Cleary, CEO of Swrve, Inc.

"Eric Mersch's book, *Hacking SaaS: An Insider's Guide to Managing Software Business Success,* is a powerful resource for investors, analysts, and any executive building a cloud-first company. He leverages his extensive experience with emerging SaaS companies to explain the operational and financial models that are foundational to the software-as-a-service industry. The book distills complex frameworks into intuitive concepts by providing rich context supported with easy-to-understand examples and target metrics. His work has been instrumental for my investment research, as it has helped me to gain a CFO's perspective into SaaS performance metrics and financial reporting. The emergence of SaaS models and the adoption of digital transformation are both trends that are still early in their development, and Eric's work provides critical tools for anyone who is managing or analyzing the businesses driving the SaaS economy."

—**Erik Suppiger, Equity Analyst at JMP Securities**

HACKING
SaaS

An Insider's Guide to Managing Software Business Success

ERIC MERSCH

HOUNDSTOOTH
PRESS

First Edition

Hardcover ISBN: 978-1-5445-4382-6
Paperback ISBN: 978-1-5445-4383-3
Ebook ISBN: 978-1-5445-4384-0

To my inspirational wife, Andi Trindle Mersch,
and my wonderful children, Alexis and Nicholas

Software-as-a-Service Definition: Software-as-a-Service refers to a business model used to offer software licensing on a subscription basis for a specific period of time with delivery from a centrally hosted location.

CONTENTS

FOREWORD

FLG Partners, a CFO and BOD advisory firm with deep roots in Silicon Valley and the Bay Area, has provided thought leadership in the New Economy for twenty years, helping both California and the national economy transition from reliance on heavy industry to a knowledge-based economy. Our partnership serves the life sciences, healthcare, consumer packaged goods and e-commerce, and hardware and software industries. Our FLG partners have helped drive success for many companies, from emerging venture capital-backed startups, to large private-equity-funded businesses, to mature public companies. And this operating and strategy experience has positioned us well to provide thought leadership in these industries. Now I'm excited to introduce our latest thought piece on Software-as-a-Service, or SaaS, by FLG Partner Eric Mersch with peer review by fellow FLG partners Ken Chow and Ron Fior.

Eric has worked with SaaS companies, private and public, for over two decades. The guidance in this book comes directly from his experience helping to drive success in these companies. During his career, he has identified a knowledge gap in SaaS management and strategy. In this book, which I believe is a definitive source of SaaS knowledge, Eric fills this gap.

Eric joined FLG Partners in 2018 bringing his wealth of SaaS experience to our firm. When I assumed the Managing Partner role in 2020, I doubled down on thought leadership initiatives. Our blog content (*FLG Perspectives*) grew at a rate of two to three articles per month and this has doubled views and increased viewing time. Eric has published nearly all of our SaaS content, which our SaaS clients reference during and after engagements.

In the past three years, we grew our partner count and footprint, adding new metropolitan areas in Los Angeles and New York, and this has brought highly experienced CFOs to our business. We look forward to many more years of helping our clients succeed through our thought leadership. Stay tuned.

—Laureen DeBuono,
Managing Partner, FLG Partners

AUTHOR'S NOTE

I spent nearly my entire business career in subscription software, from the dot-com days to the 2020s and experienced the growth of the industry firsthand. When I moved up to the CFO role, I recognized the strategic importance of the SaaS business model and learned how to manage these businesses. After my last public company CFO role as a full-time employee, I started working as an interim CFO so that I could engage with as many SaaS companies as possible, thus accelerating my learning. Through this experience, I gained operational knowledge and learned to connect operations with company strategy.

I found that learning the SaaS business model was challenging because of the lack of credible educational resources. David Skok's online lectures and website, www.forentrepreneurs.com, was helpful. There are valuable blogs out there, but the message is diluted by the massive amount of online content. The industry lacked a resource that provided an education about the business model.

Based on the insight I developed, I started writing articles on best-in-class SaaS management. When I joined FLG Partners in 2018, I resolved to write a book with the key objective of offering the industry a single resource that consolidates knowledge on the SaaS business model, describes a framework for classifying iterations on these business models and provides a standardized methodology for managing SaaS companies. I wanted to give guidance on defining, measuring, and executing on SaaS metrics, but I wanted to inform the industry that operational activities must support strategy, for it is the strategy that provides the most value to the company.

It was hard to find the time to write with a full slate of clients and family commitments. Then, life threw me a curveball when I was diagnosed with advanced prostate cancer in March 2022. At the time, my doctors gave me one to three years to live. As you can imagine, I was completely devastated. I transitioned off my clients as quickly as possible to spend more time with family and focus on my health. And I needed to prepare for the upcoming treatments, which I expected to be strenuous (and indeed they were).

My diagnosis gave me added motivation to complete the book. I wanted to inspire my children with wisdom to help them in their own lives regardless of their future career choices and to emphasize the importance of lifelong learning. And I felt the need to achieve a lofty goal of adding to our collective human knowledge, even in a niche subject.

So when I sat down to write the book, I had about 30,000 words of content with which to work. Updating the content, writing transition sections took most of the summer and fall of 2022. The wonderful people at Scribe Media helped restructure my raw manuscript into a true business book. I finally finished all edits in the winter of 2023 and published shortly thereafter.

Nearly one year after my diagnosis, following months of treatment, I'm happy to announce that my outlook has improved significantly. I now expect to live many years and will use the time to be a good husband, father, friend, and business executive.

—Eric Mersch,
San Francisco

PART 1

SAAS 101

Several years ago, I was in conversation with a fellow experienced technology Chief Financial Officer (CFO). My colleague stated flatly that selling software subscriptions was not new, saying that the SaaS business model was like that of newspapers. Now, I very much respect this person as a CFO but was surprised by this statement. By that time, I had fifteen years of CFO experience with SaaS companies and had developed a very different opinion. However, it was a valuable conversation because it taught me that if a CFO of such experience does not understand the true value of the SaaS business model, then many others will likely share this opinion.

Let's explore the newspaper metaphor and consider printed editions for now. The only commonality is in the billing methodology. Readers pay a monthly fee and get a month's worth of information. SaaS software customers pay a monthly fee and get to use the software for that month. The newspaper company has no insight into the reader's behavior. The paper is delivered to an individual customer at an address. And that is all the newspaper company knows. The SaaS company watches the customer's interaction with its software in real time and can derive insights from this behavior.

So to complete the metaphor, the printed edition would need to arrive at the reader's home with a newspaper employee in attendance throughout the day. This employee would observe the reader's engagement with the newspaper. When does the person read the newspaper? And for how long? What reading format works best? Which articles are of interest? Which advertisements provoke action? Further, the employee would suggest, in real time, other articles and advertisements that would be of interest to the reader. At the end of the day, the employee would provide notes on the reader's behavior to the newspaper editor who would change the next day's newspaper's content and format to suit the reader's personal reading habits. Each subsequent day would bring improved content personalized for an individual reader.

Hopefully, you see that such a newspaper business model could not possibly work. After all, the business would need one employee for each individual reader to understand the customer behavior for millions of customers. However, SaaS companies operate the software directly through a cloud provider and can thus observe customers' interaction automatically without assigning one employee to observe each customer.

SaaS companies track customer usage in real time for any segment of users down to a single individual. By parsing the behavioral data, companies continually increase the value of the software to the end users. Software features and functionality can be updated rapidly to increase the end users' productivity. The addition of new software features can support new use cases not contemplated in the original release. Training tutorials served up at the right moment can increase engagement by training end users, helping them to get more out of the software.

Updating the analogy with a digital media news company helps with the comparison because the company can observe popular articles and track digital advertising performance. But it still falls short because digital media is passively consumed. SaaS companies provide digitized workflows that enhance productivity for consumers and companies. The software customers' end users actively engage with the SaaS software to complete their jobs more quickly and with better outcomes.

The main takeaway from this metaphor is that the SaaS business model is not about just selling software with a subscription license. With customer behavior insight, SaaS companies can innovate their software faster than non-SaaS businesses.

An Introduction to the Book

In this book, we will explore the organization of SaaS companies, their financial profile, and the metrics we use to manage success.

In **Part 1**, we will dive deeper into the differences between SaaS and perpetual business models, exploring the history of each business model and identifying the key characteristics that influenced the rise of SaaS.

Then we will discuss the key SaaS metrics and how we use them to maximize performance of the SaaS business model. Many of these metrics are linked to the financial profile, which is the term I use to describe the three standard financial statements—the balance sheet, the income statement, and the cash flow statement. We'll review the three categories of SaaS metrics, which I define as *Top Line, Unit Economics,* and *Financial.* Then we'll develop a five-year financial model for a theoretical SaaS company. This exercise will help you link the three categories of metrics and understand the power of benchmarking in managing success in your SaaS business.

We will finish Part 1 with an overview of how we use SaaS metrics in strategic planning and tactical operations.

In **Parts 2 and 3**, we will take an in-depth look at specific groupings of SaaS models with similar financial profiles and learn two ways in which to evaluate SaaS models. In Part 2, we will focus on a Customer-Centric model in which the SaaS company is defined by its target customer and includes three subsets: Enterprise SaaS models, Small to Mid-Market (SMM) SaaS models, and Business-to-Consumer (B2C) SaaS models. In Part 3, we'll look at an Industry-Centric model, which, as the name suggests, is based on the specific industry served. We will learn why the specific type of SaaS model under this classification scheme requires a specific operating structure and, hence, financial profile. Using these business model classifications for your SaaS company will allow you to best understand and manage your business both strategically and tactically.

Reading this book requires focused study. But by doing so, you will position yourself for success in managing the SaaS business model.

CHAPTER 1

SAAS VERSUS PERPETUAL MODELS

The Perpetual Software License Model

Until the late 1990s, all software was sold as a perpetual license, meaning the customer purchases the software with the right to use it indefinitely. Microsoft is the prime example. Customers purchased the MS Office productivity suite on CD-ROM disk at a local computer store and installed it on their computers. The product came with a book to explain the functionality and there was a help desk phone number if one was desperate. But the software was intuitive, and most customers started using the software out of the box. Microsoft had little insight on customers' engagement with the software. Product managers observed customer behavior of focus groups from behind one-way mirrors and took and passed notes to engineers in subsequent meetings. Sometimes the customer feedback made its way into the software and sometimes not. Sometimes engineers added features that customers found useless or annoying or both. Early software features such as "Microsoft Bob" and "Clippy" are two great examples of updates that no one wanted. Such focus groups were the only information Microsoft had on customer behavior.

Later, to augment focus groups, Microsoft recruited end users to install a type of tracking software that recorded their keystrokes while they were using the MS Office product. The company mailed these volunteers CD-ROMs with the tracking software and a return envelope. After a period of time, the end users mailed the disks back to the company which presumably used the information to update the software. The physical exchange of information from a small sample set of users on their interaction with the software several months earlier made for a very slow and inefficient innovation cycle.

Let's stay with the Microsoft example to highlight other characteristics of the Perpetual Software License model. Customers who purchase a certain version of the software have the right to use it indefinitely but do not have rights to newer versions. Microsoft made upgrades available periodically and customers needed to purchase this version to access the most current features and functionality. The long innovation cycle meant that major upgrades could take years. And the upgrades that were ultimately released were packed with hundreds of new features designed to meet every use case no matter how unique. Most end users found that the vast majority of new features were irrelevant. For some users, it took years to discover a version's new features, usually through word of mouth or even accidentally.

Bulky software upgrades also required computer hardware with greater processing power. Although some customers enjoyed buying the latest and greatest computers, customers typically had a negative reaction to the need to purchase new hardware to run new versions that were only incrementally better. Some customers using older versions did not see the need to buy a new computer to run the newest software versions. Thus, the new software versions served as a natural barrier to adoption for existing customers. The cost of new computer hardware is still a characteristic of the Perpetual Software License model today as is the need to maintain the increasingly complex hardware infrastructure required.

Accessing customer support is always seen as a challenging issue by customers. In the Perpetual Software License model, there is a good reason for this. Since companies earn the vast majority of their revenue from a specific software version at the point of sale, there is no incentive to provide robust customer support. Customers live with this frustration because of the high cost of switching to another software option. However, the lack of customer support leaves the perpetual software company vulnerable to disruption. On the company side, limiting customer support also limits the opportunity to collect data on the customer experience. Remember, knowledge of customer behavior is an important driver of innovation. On the customer side, frustration with the business model opened opportunities for startup SaaS companies to steal customers.

The SaaS Model

The SaaS business model is one in which the software is licensed on a subscription basis for a specific period of time and delivered from a centrally hosted location, often by a third-party cloud computing company, and operated by the SaaS company.

Today, the SaaS business model is the dominant approach for providing software to end users. There are some companies that sell perpetual software, but nearly all new software companies use the SaaS model. And companies that operate a Perpetual Software License model are actively transitioning to SaaS. It's unlikely that today's college graduates will encounter perpetual software in their careers. This fact of life serves as the rationale for my book, and this is to teach people how to manage SaaS business models.

Early SaaS companies arose in the late 1990s as venture-backed companies sought new ways to deliver software products. At the time, these new companies, called Application Service Providers, or ASPs, focused on offering the internet infrastructure, i.e., providing computers, data center facilities, and networks, through which they deployed third-party software to customers who paid a recurring fee. One of these early companies was Corio, which purchased software from vendors such as Oracle, Siebel, and SAP to host and rent to customers. The target market consisted of larger corporations with tens to hundreds of employees who would use the software, i.e., the end users.

The state of technology at that time did not allow for the fast interaction between the end users and today's hosted software. Corio used a technology called an *inline frame*, colloquially referred to as *iFrame*, that allowed software users to interact with third-party software hosted remotely.

iFrame technology was a major innovation in that it allowed for end users to remotely access software. This was cutting-edge technology at the time, but it had significant performance limits. The main challenge was in the end user interaction. To make remote software access work, each software button had to be tagged with an HTML code. When end users clicked on a software button, the HTML code opened a new browser tab with the next set of features. Active users often worked with dozens of open web page tabs and would need to switch back and forth to make the software function.

The lack of internet infrastructure, specifically the fiber-optic cable capacity, also hampered the end user experience. Visually, the image of the software application looked grainy because bandwidth constraints limited the pixels that could be displayed to the user. ASPs quickly faded as the dot-com boom unraveled, but ASPs proved that the technology could work.

Within five years of the April 2000 dot–com crash, the stage was set for the first true SaaS companies. The dramatic growth in information bandwidth capacity, advances in cloud computing, and the development of cloud native software architecture allowed new companies to launch quickly with lower costs and to offer a user experience equivalent to that of perpetual software. Investor dollars flowed to thousands of SaaS startups that focused on building software-based productivity tools. Existing perpetual software companies began shifting their business to the SaaS model.

Over two decades later, the SaaS business model is the dominant software delivery method in use today. The operational benefits are the inverse of the cons of the perpetual business model. Customers of SaaS companies experience ease of onboarding and operations. With the software hosted in the cloud and managed by the software provider, customers do not need to incur capital expenditure costs. High-speed internet connectivity is ubiquitous, allowing for fast connections between the hosted software and the end users. Software upgrades are released directly to the production environment in a way that is completely transparent to the customers who can begin using the upgraded features immediately.

There are financial benefits as well. The SaaS subscription model can generate a predictable recurring revenue stream that reduces financial risk. The company can staff the business with a high degree of probability that the future revenue will offset the expenses. Equity investors can better evaluate future performance and the ability to do so derisks the investment. As a result, SaaS companies can achieve higher valuations. Debt investors lend to the company with the recurring revenue as the collateral.

Compared to perpetual software companies, SaaS companies need a completely new business organization to successfully manage the software delivery. These companies incur higher costs of revenue due to the infrastructure required for software delivery—mainly bandwidth, computing power, and data storage—as well as a platform operations team to manage the whole thing. Software development is monetized over time through subscriptions instead of a one-time up-front payment and this requires higher working capital. Because customers can cancel more easily, SaaS companies developed robust customer support teams to better service customers and customer success organizations to increase customer engagement and thus ensure customer loyalty.

In return for these new challenges, SaaS companies gained access to customer behavior data. Product marketing teams mined this data for insights that drove the next phase of software development. Engineers combined these insights with the latest thinking on software development to make frequent upgrades based on these customers' insights. In this way, the product innovation cycle turned faster than ever before for software companies.

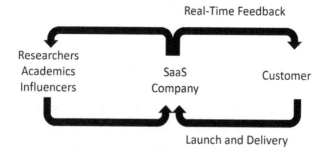

Faster innovation led to better software products and, ultimately, higher productivity among customers. Worker productivity is a key factor in economic growth as measured by the change in Gross Domestic Product (GDP). The rise of SaaS has played a key role in driving GDP growth.

Key Takeaways

Until the late 1990s, all software was sold as a perpetual license, meaning the customer purchased the software with the right to use it indefinitely. Now, almost all new software uses a SaaS model, meaning it is sold on a subscription basis. Below are the key characteristics of the Perpetual Software License and the SaaS models. Note the differences in delivery of the software because this feature of SaaS serves as a powerful differentiator between the two models.

Software licensed under the Perpetual Software License model:

- Entails a one-time fee for unlimited lifetime use but includes no right to upgrades

- Software upgrades had to be paid for separately, either in the form of additional one-time fees or as part of a maintenance contract

- Requires software to be downloaded and run on location, known as "on-premise" software

- Requires capital expenditures by customer

- Operates with little or no internet connectivity

- Provides little to no access to customer usage data

- Includes limited customer support because the vendor has no incentive to provide it

- Requires new downloads for any upgrades

Subscription software under the SaaS model:

- Offers recurring fees

- Is delivered via a centrally hosted platform typically owned and operated by a cloud computing platform company such as Amazon Web Services (AWS) or Microsoft Azure

- Requires no capital expenditures but does require robust internet connectivity

- Provides access to customer usage data in real time

- Requires robust customer support (customer support + customer success) to retain and upsell customers

- Delivers upgrades automatically without customer action

- Requires minimal or no internal operations and maintenance support

CHAPTER 2

UNDERSTANDING FINANCIAL REPORTING FOR SAAS COMPANIES

As we move into our detailed discussion of SaaS models, you will need a functional understanding of financial reporting and finance terminology. Understanding this section will enable you to connect the SaaS metric performance to the company's strategy. And this knowledge will help you serve as a true strategic advisor and business partner to the board, the Chief Executive Officer (CEO), and the management team.

You may have noticed that companies increasingly seek to educate their employees on financial reporting and incorporate an understanding of financial metrics into the company's culture. One reason is that there is so much more operational data available in today's companies. We can use this information to drive operations and strategies that allow us to outperform competitors. To use the information, though, we need to educate employees on the understanding of financial reporting standards. Only with an understanding of this common language can employees truly collaborate in a way that drives competitiveness.

Over the past twenty-some years, the adoption of systems and collection of internal data generated within companies has grown exponentially. Today, more than ever, companies use data on business activities—customer behavior, end user engagement, product innovation, monetization strategies, and internal process flows—to drive decision making. Working in SaaS companies puts you in a position to connect these operational data points to business performance and thereby improve business intelligence. The stronger the data-driven culture, the better the business performance.

For the remainder of this section, I will provide you with the basics of financial reporting and review the financial profile for SaaS companies.

Best-Practice Financial Reporting Methodologies

The primary basis for presentation of financial reports is governed by a set of accounting rules referred to as the Generally Accepted Accounting Principles, or GAAP, for US entities, or International Financial Reporting Standards, or IFRS, for entities based outside the United States. GAAP/IFRS defines the way in which accounting recognizes the company's revenue and costs, assets and liabilities, and the equity in the business.

In addition to these accounting standards, investors and creditors expect to see three types of financial statements:

- Income Statement

- Balance Sheet

- Cash Flow Statement

In this chapter, we will discuss these statements, show best practice for reporting, and define the major terms included in each. Then, as sort of a practical exercise, we will review SaaS company financial reports and highlight the specific financial profile associated with these businesses. For reference on specific terms during your reading, please see our SaaS Glossary.

FINANCIAL STATEMENTS

INCOME STATEMENT
The Income Statement is also called a Statement of Operations in public company reporting. Smaller companies may just call it a Profit and Loss Statement. The main function of the income statement is to show the revenue and costs for a specific period and the resulting profit or loss from business operations.

Best practice for income statement format is what's known as a "Multi-Step" format in that revenue and costs are organized into categories to provide for better decision making. The use of a standard format also allows for benchmarking, or the practice of comparing performance of different companies.

Revenue—The income statement starts with revenue, which is the income earned from operating the business. For SaaS companies, revenue is subdivided into:

- **Recurring software revenues**—subscription revenues from the delivery of a cloud-hosted product

- **Recurring service revenue**—revenue generated by maintenance and support contracts

- **Non-recurring revenues**—revenues typically derived from professional services work for the onboarding of new customers and that include activities such as implementation, system integration, and end user enablement

Cost of Revenue (COR)—COR (also known as Cost of Goods Sold, or COGS, in companies that sell hardware or physical products) represents the costs associated with the delivery of the hosted software product. Such costs are known as direct costs because they are incurred by directly providing the product in the period when the revenue is earned. Direct costs for SaaS companies include:

- Hosting and infrastructure

- Customer support

- Cloud operations/platform support

- Third-party software and data fees

The net of Revenue and Cost of Revenue is **Gross Profit.** **Gross Margin** is Gross Profit as a percentage of Revenue (for more on this, see Part 2).

Revenue - Cost of Revenue = Gross Profit

Gross Margin = Gross Profit ÷ Revenue

Operating Expense—Operating Expense represents the costs associated with engineering and product development, sales, customer success, marketing and business development, and administrative functions required to support the business. SaaS companies typically use three cost centers, or categories, for financial reporting. These are:

- **Research and Development**—The people and systems expenses associated with engineering and product development activities.

- **Sales and Marketing**—The people and systems expenses associated with sales, customer success, and marketing activities. Sales commissions, although based on new customers, should be included here as well.

- **General and Administrative**—These costs are associated with the people—employees, contractors, and vendors—who manage finance, accounting, legal, human resources, and facilities.

Operating Income—Operating Income is defined as Gross Profit less Operating Expense. In other words:

Gross Profit − Operating Expense = Operating Income

Net Income—Net Income equals Operating Income less expenses such as interest received on cash holdings net of interest paid on debt. These are called non-operating expenses because they are not related to the core activities of the business. One-time gains and losses from the sale of assets are included in non-operating expenses.

Adjusted EBITDA—Adjusted EBITDA reflects the company's true profitability because it excludes non-cash and non-operating expenses. EBITDA stands for Earnings Before Interest, Taxes, and Depreciation and Amortization. Non-cash expenses include:

1. Depreciation of long-lived physical assets such as computer servers

2. Amortization of soft assets such as software development and goodwill.

3. Stock-based compensation

The income statement components look like the image below on any financial report:

Revenue - Cost of Revenue = Gross Profit

Gross Margin = Gross Profit ÷ Revenue

Gross Profit - Operating Expenses = Operating Income
$$\left\{\begin{array}{l}\text{• Research and Development} \\ \text{• Sales and Marketing} \\ \text{• General and Administrative}\end{array}\right\}$$

Operating - Non-Operating = Net Income
Income   Expenses

Net Income + Non-Cash/ = Adjusted EBITDA
Non-Operating
Expense

BALANCE SHEET
The Balance Sheet is a snapshot of the company's assets and liabilities at a specific point in time. Finance produces a balance

sheet for the end of the month. For purposes of this discussion, the main Balance Sheet terms are:

Assets are simply the company's cash, money due from customers (formally, the company's accounts receivable), prepaid expenses, e.g., payments for future events such as marketing shows or professional services paid in advance.

Liabilities mainly represent the money that the company owes to vendors and suppliers (formally accounts payable) and deferred revenue. The deferred revenue balance is material in Enterprise SaaS companies because these companies receive up-front payments for software delivery in future periods. The greater the value of the up-front payments, either by charging a higher price or requiring a longer contract term, the higher the deferred revenue balance. Therefore, deferred revenue is an indication of future business performance, especially when tracked over time.

Equity is the value of the company after liabilities are subtracted. This account keeps track of venture investments as well as the operating gains or losses from the core business. A company that operates at a loss will have negative equity. This is common in venture capital companies because they consume cash well before they generate revenue growth. We will review cash flow in the next section.

One final important lesson is that the company's Assets will always equal the sum of Liabilities and Equity. This principle is known as the Accounting Equation.

Accounting Equation: Liabilities + Equity = Assets

CASH FLOW STATEMENT

The cash flow statement is the net of cash received and cash paid out by the business for working capital needs, capital investments, and financing. Thus, there are three components to the Cash Flow Statement.

Cash flow due to Operating Activities—For our discussion, this is the most important category. Operating Activities refer to the cash flow generated or consumed by the core business. The main component here is Working Capital, which we define as the money required to run the business. Working Capital amounts increase as companies incur expenses to drive future revenue. In other words, the company needs investment in the current period to acquire customers and generate cash receipts in future periods. Enterprise SaaS companies can generate negative Working Capital, which means that customer payments are made in advance of providing services. The negative term means that up-front payments actually fund some portion of the business, but this is only true if the company is growing.

Cash flow due to Investing Activities—This cash flow category is defined as money spent to acquire hardware to support customers and employees. Companies that build and operate their own data centers will have large investments. Most SaaS companies today use third-party data centers such as Amazon Web Services, Microsoft Azure, Google Cloud Platform, and Oracle Cloud; these are classified in Operating Expense. So the only cash flow items from investing activities for these companies are employee laptops, networking equipment, and office furniture.

Cash flow due to Financing Activities—These are cash flows from equity investments and assumption of debt. Venture investments are equity. Bank loans are debt.

FREE CASH FLOW

The Free Cash Flow metric is the single most important line item in financial reporting. It is the true measure of the cash generated or consumed by the business. The sum of Cash Flow from Operating Activities and Investing Activities is the company's Free Cash Flow, or FCF. When private companies report their Burn, or Burn Rate, they are referring to the company's Free Cash Flow. Venture-backed companies almost always have negative Free Cash Flow because they are using investments to build and deploy products into new markets on the bet that they can emerge as a profitable market leader.

Cash flow from operating activities +
cash flow from investing activities = Free Cash Flow

One important point about SaaS company Free Cash Flow is that Operating Income is not a proxy for Free Cash Flow. In SaaS companies that sell low-price-point software applications to consumers on a monthly basis, the up-front cost to acquire customers reduces cash flow as the customer base grows. The faster the growth (inorganic, meaning that the company pays for new users), the greater the negative cash flow. We call this dynamic the Working Capital Trough (see Chapter 10).

In SaaS companies that sell high-price-point software applications to large corporations, the purchase price is invoiced annually at the start of the twelve-month contract. The full annual subscription is received up front (although with some collections delay), while the subscription revenue is recognized over twelve months. The ratable recognition of subscription revenue means that Operating Income will generally be smooth over the same period. Thus, operating income trends do not follow the cash flow in this situation.

In both cases, Operating Income differs from Free Cash Flow.

Key Takeaways

Investors and creditors expect to see three types of financial statements:

- The Income Statement (also called Statement of Operations or Profit and Loss Statement) shows the revenue and costs for a specific period and the resulting profit or loss.

- The Balance Sheet shows a company's assets, liabilities, and equity assets at a specific point in time (usually the end of the month).

- The Cash Flow Statement shows cash received and cash paid out by the business due to operating, investing, and financing activities.

Understanding the details of financial statements in the context of best-practice reporting is critical because it serves to provide a common language among operators and investors.

CHAPTER 3

TOP-LINE METRICS

There are three categories of SaaS metrics: **Top-Line, Unit Economic,** and **Financial** metrics. **Top-Line** metrics are key performance indicators (KPIs) that describe the company's earliest revenue activity. Once the customer signs a contract, we use a number of metrics to describe the value of this specific customer and the health of the company in aggregate. The **Top-Line** metrics are not defined by GAAP or IFRS, and therefore are Non-GAAP/Non-IFRS metrics.

Top-Line metrics are most applicable to companies that sell high-dollar complex software to large enterprises. We refer to such companies as Enterprise SaaS companies (more on these in Part 2).

Note that Top-Line metrics are based on Software Subscription Revenue only—they do not include revenue from services related to the software!

The financial profile of Software Subscription Revenue is very different from that of services revenue. Specifically, the gross margins differ greatly. Software Subscription Revenue requires little direct costs to host and deliver and thus generates gross margins in the high 70% range. Services are priced at low margins, typically in the range of 20%–40%, and thus look, from a financial perspective, like a different type of revenue.

Some companies bundle service revenue with Software Subscription Revenue for financial and SaaS metric reporting.

To understand the reasoning, we need to understand the non-recurring and recurring activities for which the company charges customers. Non-recurring activities are related to onboarding of new customers. These non-recurring activities include integrating the software with customers' existing technology and training the customers' end users. Customers pay a one-time fee for implementation and the SaaS company records services revenue during the time it is earned. Recurring activities include maintenance and support services and these are typically included in the contract as a subscription fee. It's the recurring services revenue that causes confusion.

Combining recurring services revenue with Software Subscription Revenue increases the total revenue of the contract and this is the reasoning companies use when adopting this methodology. Although revenue is higher, the combined gross margin will be much lower than that of the Software Subscription Revenue. The total revenue may be more impressive at first look, but deeper analysis will show that the combined revenue stream is not as valuable as that of other comparable companies. Gross margin calculated this way will significantly lag that of industry benchmarks.

Finally, company stakeholders—investors, debtors, board members, executives, and employees—will expect Top-Line metrics to reflect the value of the Software Subscription Revenue only. Adding recurring or non-recurring revenue to the Top-Line metrics will be confusing and, ultimately, will hurt your credibility as a SaaS professional.

Annual Contract Value (ACV)

The most important of all Top-Line metrics is the ACV because it serves as the basis for all other Top-Line metrics. All others are derived from this important concept.

The ACV is the annual value of a customer's Subscription Revenue only. It is the annual fee a company charges the customer for access to the software and is defined in the contract. When we look at the business as a whole, we report average ACV, which is the average value of all customer contracts.

We also use ACV as a means of classifying SaaS companies in the Customer-Centric model (see Part 2). Enterprise SaaS companies have higher average ACVs than do those companies that serve individual consumers (i.e., B2C, and those that serve Small to Mid-Market companies). Higher average ACV products reflect a more robust software product and this means that the financial profile of the company will differ from that of a low-average ACV product. Thus, we need to look at a company's average ACV to best understand the business.

Total Contract Value (TCV)

The TCV is the total value of the contract's Subscription Revenue measured over the life of the contract regardless of the billing terms. As an example, consider that a two-year contract has a TCV that is twice the amount of its ACV assuming that the second year does not include discounts or price increases. The specific invoicing terms for this contract do not impact TCV. In this two-year contract example, billing terms for Enterprise SaaS companies typically require an up-front payment for the first year or an up-front payment for the two years. Regardless, the TCV will be the same in both scenarios. Note that the calculation may change slightly if the contract includes annual price increases.

If, in our example, the price for the second year of the contract increases by 20%, then the TCV will be 2.2x the ACV. For reporting purposes, a useful metric is the ratio of TCV to ACV. The higher the ratio, the "stickier" the customer base, leading to retention improvements and a more efficient sales cycle.

Annual Recurring Revenue (ARR)

We define ARR as the annual Software Subscription Revenue run rate of an individual contract or all contracts in aggregate with revenue in a given period. The simple way to calculate ARR is by multiplying the current month's revenue by 12.

Note that the ARR may differ from ACV due to timing differences. For example, let's look at an example of a company that signs a $120,000 ACV contract. However, it may take the company some months to get the customer operational on the software. Operational means that the software is fully integrated with the customer's other systems and all designated users have the access and the know-how to use the software. This point at which the customer is operational is referred to as "customer activation" and the contract is referred to as an active contract. And the time between the signing of the contract and the customer activation date is referred to as "Time to Go Live" or "Time to Live" and is written as "TTL." Thus, a $120,000 ACV contract signed on March 31, 2023 may not generate $120,000 in ARR until later in the year.

Timing differences are common for Enterprise SaaS companies because these companies sell high-dollar complex software that requires long implementation cycles.

Differences also occur when the customer wants the contract to start on some specific future date. I see this customer behavior when selling into large companies with annual budgets: the buyer may need to wait for new budget funds in the next fiscal year. This is often true with government agencies. So a $120,000 ACV contract signed on March 31, 2023, may not generate $120,000 in ARR until October 1, 2023, which is the start of the US government's fiscal year.

Finally, contracts with start dates after the first of the month will have revenue prorated for the number of days active in that month. A $120,000 ACV contract that starts mid-month will generate only $5,000 for that first month. So the $120,000 ACV contract will generate $60,000 in ARR for that specific month ($5,000 × 12 months) and the subsequent month's ARR will increase to $120,000 ($10,000 × 12 months).

Contracted Annual Recurring Revenue (CARR)

CARR is the subscription revenue of a given period calculated as an annual run rate for all active contracts *plus* those that are signed but not yet active. CARR differs from ARR for two main reasons:

- CARR includes the ARR of new customers who are not yet live because the customer onboarding process is not yet complete. The time it takes to get the customer live (TTL as discussed) is a function of the company's ability to onboard new customers efficiently, but the customer's preparedness and commitment may drive timing as well. So TTL is not entirely within the company's control. This dynamic makes CARR a more accurate KPI for reporting Subscription Recurring Revenue.

- Using CARR avoids the step function changes in ARR. These changes are driven by the TTL in that revenue cannot be recognized until the customer is live, the date of which is referred to as the Go Live, thus meeting the GAAP revenue recognition criteria for delivery. The contract will not generate revenue until the period of the Go Live date and will accumulate in deferred revenue during this time.

Then, in the period of the Go Live date, all of the deferred revenue for this contract will be booked and this will increase the monthly subscription revenue for this customer by the number of months of deferred revenue. In the subsequent period, revenue will drop back down to the monthly subscription revenue. As an example, a new customer with a $120,000 ACV contract, which requires a three-month TTL, will have a monthly revenue pattern of zero for the first three months, $40,000 in the fourth month, and $10,000 in the fifth month and all subsequent months. This dynamic introduces volatility into the ARR metric. This is why CARR is the preferred metric for Enterprise SaaS companies.

Monthly Recurring Revenue (MRR)—MRR is simply one-twelfth of a company's ARR. Companies with smaller ACV products such as those that sell to consumers will use MRR in addition to ARR because the customer base changes significantly from month to month.

Committed Monthly Recurring Revenue (CMRR)—CMRR, pronounced "see-mer," is the MRR that is under a contract term greater than one month. Put another way, all MRR under quarterly or annual contracts is referred to as CMMR. Customers under longer term contracts have longer customer lifetimes and this makes them more valuable.

CMMR is a common metric for Small/Mid-Market (SMM) and Business-to-Consumer (B2C) companies because they typically offer a mix of monthly, quarterly, and annual contracts unlike Enterprise SaaS companies for which annual contracts are standard. CMMR and MRR are reported together, sometimes just with CMMR as a percentage of total MRR, and the difference between the two provides insight into the stability of the consumer base. For example, a company with 80% CMRR to total MRR has a more stable consumer base than one with 20% because fewer customers can churn in any given month.

Available ARR/Exposed Annual Recurring Revenue (Exposed ARR)—In any given time period—a month, a quarter, or a year—some percentage of the company's customer contracts expire. SaaS companies rely heavily on customer renewals and thus need to track expiring contracts closely. The metric we typically use to track expiring contracts is Exposed ARR or Available ARR. Investors tend to use the term "Exposed ARR" due to the risk that expiring contracts pose for the company. Internal to the company, I like to use the term "Available ARR" to reflect the opportunity to upsell the customer; I find that this is a more positive approach than using Exposed ARR. Another term you may see is Expiring ARR, but this is less common.

The specific definition of whichever of the two terms you use is the ARR of all contracts expiring in a given period and that are available to renew. I use ARR for this metric as opposed to CARR because customers will certainly be active by the time of the contract expiration date (although I have seen otherwise). The ARR lost due to customers who do not renew is referred to as churn. We track churn closely because it indicates the value of the software to the customers and because we need to retain the revenue to earn back the costs of acquiring the customer—we need to earn a return on investment for acquiring new customers.

Bookings

The term "Bookings" refers to the annual aggregate value of all contracts signed in a given time period. Bookings differ from the ACV and TCV terms, which are based on a single contract. For example, we refer to the value of all contracts signed in a given fiscal quarter as that quarter's Bookings.

Bookings related to a specific contract should only be reported if we assess that this contract will convert to revenue with a high degree of probability. Revenue recognition rules do not apply to Bookings because the timing is based on contract signature date and not on the date that GAAP/IFRS rules allow us to recognize revenue. The contract may not convert to revenue if we fail to successfully onboard the customer. Therefore, you will need to assess such risks before deciding to report Bookings. Having to reduce the Bookings number as reported in prior fiscal periods is embarrassing for all involved and hurts the credibility of the financial reporting process.

We use the Bookings term for both the recurring and non-recurring contract value in addition to Software Subscription contract value. For example, we may have $100 million in Bookings for our first fiscal quarter and this amount includes $70 million of Software Subscription, $20 million in Professional Services (non-recurring), and $10 million in customer support (recurring). These Bookings will generate $100 million in revenue over an annual period. Designating the Bookings as Subscription, Recurring, and Non-Recurring provides us insight into the value by revenue type and the time periods over which the revenue will be recognized.

And we use this term to report on changes in aggregate contract value over time. For example, the addition of new customers, the loss of existing customers, and changes in value—higher and lower—all have separate designations. We use Subscription

Bookings for Software Subscription Revenue and Recurring Bookings.

Subscription Bookings—At the highest level, the Subscription Bookings metric is defined as the ACV of a contract's Subscription Revenue. We use annual values because all Go-To-Market (GTM) benchmarks are expressed in annual values. Investors will always view the company's metrics on an annual basis. And operators manage the business on an annual time period. Budgets are created for a given fiscal year. Sales Incentive Plans (SIPs) are based on annual quotas with annual attainment milestones for payments. We report Subscription Bookings separate from all other revenue streams because this revenue is the most critical to the success of the business.

Recurring Bookings—This is a term for the ACV of all recurring services contracts, specifically Maintenance and Support revenue. Typically, a SaaS company, especially Enterprise SaaS companies, provide such services throughout the contract term.

Non-Recurring Bookings—This is the dollar value of all contracts for non-recurring revenue, which includes professional services, perpetual software license sales, and hardware sales. Because these types of sales do not extend for more than one year, we don't use annual bases.

Professional services for implementation and integration and training are the most common types of Non-Recurring Bookings. Enterprise SaaS companies offer complex software platforms, which typically require professional services for software implementation and training. The pricing of these services are based on the professional service hours performed. Since these are one-time offerings, we consider them to be non-recurring. Cybersecurity company CrowdStrike serves as a good example. This company reports both subscription, i.e., recurring, and professional services, i.e., non-recurring.

Many software companies are in the process of transitioning to a SaaS business model. These companies sell their software on a subscription basis as well as a perpetual license. In these cases, such companies will report subscription software and perpetual license software sales separately. For example, Development Operations (DevOps) Platform provider JFrog uses two financial reporting categories for revenue: *Subscription-self-managed and SaaS* and *License-self-managed*. The first category refers to subscription revenue; the second category refers to revenue derived from the sale of perpetual software licenses.

There are also many companies transitioning from a hardware and perpetual software business model to a subscription model. For example, Nutanix, a provider of software solutions and cloud services that enable enterprise infrastructure operations, has three non-recurring revenue line items—perpetual software licenses, hardware appliances (hardware that ships to the customer with the software preloaded), and professional services. Nutanix serves as a good example of a company that has transitioned to a SaaS model. Fiscal year 2022 perpetual license revenue was only 5% of total revenue versus 47% in fiscal year 2018.

Total Subscription Bookings—The ACV of both New Subscription Bookings and Renewal Subscription Bookings. We report these two Bookings types separately because the cost to acquire these Bookings differ widely. It's much more expensive to acquire a new customer than to renew an existing customer. In my experience, the cost to renew customers, and thus generate Renewal Bookings, can be as low as one-fifth of New Bookings.

New Subscription Bookings—The ACV of New Customer Subscription Bookings and Expansion Subscription Bookings as measured on the contract signature date, i.e., the Bookings Date. Best-in-class SaaS companies increase subscription revenue in two ways. The first is by adding new customers. The second is by selling more software subscriptions to existing customers. Thus, New Subscription Bookings include both.

New Customer Subscription Bookings—The ACV of Bookings from new customers acquired by the business as measured on the contract signature date. New customers are often referred to as "New Logos," meaning that the new customers have not had a prior relationship with your company. New customers may expand the dollar value of their original ACV soon after the initial purchase. When the expansion occurs within the same quarter of the original Booking (as defined by the contract date), the incremental ACV is typically referred to as "Fast-Follow Subscription Bookings" and this ACV is included as New Customer Subscription Bookings. Expansion of new contracts that occur after the initial quarter are referred to as such.

Expansion Subscription Bookings—The ACV of new subscriptions sold to an existing customer after the quarter of initial Bookings date. Expansion Subscription Bookings are classified as either Upsell or Cross-Sell Bookings.

- **Upsell Subscription Bookings**—The ACV of contracts that increase an existing customer's utilization of the original product. Adding more seat licenses or moving a customer to a higher usage tier are examples of Upsell Subscription Bookings.

- **Cross-Sell Subscription Bookings**—The ACV of contracts that result in the sale of related or complementary software or services subscriptions to an existing customer. The sale of additional software features is an example of Cross-Sell Subscription Bookings.

Fast-Follow Subscription Bookings—The ACV of a Subscription Booking for an existing customer and that occurs in the same quarter as that of the initial contract date. Fast-Follow Bookings count as New Bookings for the purpose of sales commission calculations and quota retirement.

Renewal Subscription Bookings—The ACV of contract renewals measured at the Renewal Date, i.e., the date of term renewal regardless of the signature date. For example, a one-year contract with a signature date of 3/15/2022 and a start date of 4/1/2022 will have a renewal date of 3/31/2023. The contract can be renewed at any point before (preferably not after!) the renewal date. But as long as the start date for the second year of the contract is 3/31/2023, Renewal Subscription Bookings are deemed to occur on this date. In this example, the Renewal Date lies in a separate quarter from the start date. In this case, the Renewal Bookings will occur in the first quarter (assuming the company's fiscal year follows the calendar year). The ACV of the Renewal Subscription Bookings will be the same as that of the original Subscription Bookings. Any increase in ACV for the subsequent year, or years, should be considered Expansion Bookings. This is true even if the original contract includes a price increase.

Reactivation Subscription Bookings—The ACV of Bookings from a prior customer that churned and was subsequently reacquired in a future period. This metric is commonly used in B2C companies that experience high churn due to low switching costs and serve a highly fragmented market. Such companies run marketing campaigns focused on churned users with specific reactivation incentives based on the consumer's behavior as an active customer. Reactivated consumers are tracked as a separate cohort within the company's revenue stream. This metric is typically expressed as Monthly Recurring Revenue when used for this purpose. In my experience, most Enterprise SaaS companies will refer to Reactivation Subscription Bookings as New Subscription Bookings because reactivation of prior customers is uncommon.

Billings

The SaaS term "Billings" refers to the invoicing terms of a contract. Specifically, Billings is the dollar value of the New or Renewal Subscription Bookings amount invoiced on the date defined by the contract terms, i.e., the Billings Date. We use Billings in addition to Bookings to provide insight into the cash flow from Bookings.

In Enterprise SaaS companies with a high-average ACV, the Billing Date typically starts on the first of the month following the month of the Bookings Date. However, the Billings Date may be delayed for several months. I've seen this in cases where the customer waits on new budget dollars from a subsequent fiscal year or has tied payment to certain milestones. In B2C SaaS companies with a low-average ACV, the Billings Date is usually the date that the customer provisions the product by registering and entering a credit card number.

Key Takeaways

We use Top-Line metrics to describe the earliest revenue activity. These metrics indicate business performance prior to the point at which the company recognizes revenue as defined by GAAP. Hence, they reside above the revenue line item and this makes them Top-Line metrics.

- ACV is the basis for all Top-Line SaaS metrics. Sales pipeline opportunities, Bookings, Billings, ARR, CARR, and sales commission all use ACV for reporting and calculation. In the following chapter on Unit Economics, you will notice the use of ACV in many metrics. Finally, it's important that ACV should only include SaaS revenue. Services revenue, even if it is recurring, should not be included in ACV.

- TCV is ACV adjusted for the contract term. We use TCV/ACV as a metric for success in gaining contract terms greater than one year. The higher the TCV/ACV ratio, the better.

- ARR equals ACV for the first year for the original contract. ARR begins at the point of revenue recognition. The greater the time between contract signing and the point at which the customer is active on the software platform, the greater the difference between Bookings and ARR.

- CARR is used when we have several months of difference between ARR and Bookings. CARR captures the true ARR of all signed contracts.

- Bookings represent the earliest concrete indication of future revenue. You must, however, be able to evaluate the probability of conversion to revenue with a high degree of accuracy. Establishing a firm evaluation process will ensure financial reporting integrity.

- Billings represent the amount of a contract's ACV that can be invoiced. The Billings metric provides insight into the cash flow. The Billings-to-Bookings ratio is a proxy for success in attaining up-front payments.

CHAPTER 4

UNIT ECONOMICS

SaaS companies have a whole set of metrics related to return on investment (ROI) and customer success. We use the term "Unit Economics" to refer to the measurement of the revenues and costs associated with an average for a specific cohort of customers with cohort typically defined as a group of customers based on month of acquisition. It's the most basic view of the business that shows the ROI in new customer acquisition. Evaluating the company's performance in this way will allow you to gain an understanding of profitability on a per-customer basis and to measure your performance with established benchmarks.

Customer Lifetime Value (CLTV) or Lifetime Value (LTV)

The CLTV is defined as the average Net Present Value of the company's average customer by cohort. The high variability and short time horizon means that we can ignore inflation for calculating this metric and treat all future dollars equally. The short time horizon also means that we calculate this metric in months instead of years. We calculate Monthly Gross Profit as the product of the Average Revenue per Account, or ARPA (also referred to as ARPU or Average Revenue per Unit) as defined by the Average ARR of the customer base and the Subscription Revenue Gross Margin. Customer Lifetime is the average tenure of a customer and is calculated as the inverse of churn rate for mature SaaS companies but often set between three and five years for early-stage companies. Thus, the CLTV of an individual customer cohort is the product of the average Monthly Gross Profit and the Customer Lifetime as shown in this CLTV equation:

$$CLTV/CAC = \frac{ARPA \times Gross\ Margin \times Customer\ Lifetime}{Customer\ Acquisition\ Cost}$$

with both the numerator and denominator expressed as the average for a cohort of new customers acquired

Gross Churn Rate—The percentage of ARR that does not renew at the contract's renewal date. For an Enterprise SaaS company, we express this metric in dollars and not customer count because the revenue impact is more closely related to change in absolute dollar churn. Hence, we refer to this as Gross Dollar Churn Rate. Small/Mid-Market and B2C SaaS companies use customer count, and we call this simply Gross Churn Rate. We can use the Gross Churn Rate to calculate the Customer Lifetime. For example, a company that loses, on average, 5% of its customer ARR each month has a twenty-month Customer Lifetime, or 1 divided by 5%. (Mathematically, a reduction in the ARR by 5% per month for a cohort of customers results in an average lifetime for all customers of 22.7565 months. But the shortcut of using the inverse of churn works well enough for our calculations.)

Retention Rate—Retention Rate is expressed either as a dollar-based metric or customer count-based metric. Enterprise and Small/Mid-Market SaaS companies use dollar-based retention because of the large variance in the customer ACV. The loss of one customer may or may not have a material impact on ARR. Contraction in one large customer contract would impact

ARR, but a count-based metric would not fully account for the magnitude of the lost ARR. Finally, these customers tend to be more stable and less likely to churn. Alternatively, B2C SaaS companies use a count-based metric because average ACV among the customer base is more similar and the customers are more likely to churn.

Renewal Rate—The existing ARR or customers that we successfully renew on the renewal date as a percentage of the total up for renewal. This metric is more common to Enterprise SaaS and Small/Mid-Market SaaS companies because a large portion of the customer base is under contract, typically annual, and therefore not eligible to churn until the contract renewal date. B2C SaaS companies rely on month-to-month contracts, so the Renewal and Retention Rates will be the same.

The Renewal Rate will always be lower than the Retention Rate because the denominator is smaller. As an example, consider a company with $250,000 of Exposed ARR in a specific quarter and this makes up 25% of its $1 million ARR base. The company renews 80% or $200,000 of this Exposed AR. The Retention Rate during this quarter is 95% or $950,000 of its $1 million ARR base. The $950,000 numerator is the sum of the Renewed ARR, $200,000, and the ARR that was not up for renewal, $750,000.

Expansion Rate—The additional recurring revenue generated from existing customers through either Upsells or Cross-sells, expressed as a percentage of existing ARR. Enterprise SaaS companies use this metric because the ACV of new customers can be expanded by capturing a larger share of their technology budgets either by selling to more users at the company or by selling more products.

Net Churn Rate—The net result of Gross Churn Rate and the Expansion Rate. Net Churn Rate is shown as a negative number.

Net Expansion Rate—The net result of Gross Churn Rate and the Expansion Rate. Net Expansion Rate is shown as a positive number.

Dollar-Based Net Retention (DBNR)—The DBNR Rate is a function of Retention Rate and Expansion Rate. This metric is used by Enterprise SaaS companies because expansion opportunities are a significant source of growth. A good DBNR for an Enterprise SaaS company is 120%, but best-in-class rates are much higher. Another common term is Net Dollar Retention, or NDR, which has the same meaning.

Customer Acquisition Cost (CAC)—The CAC is the average cost to acquire a new customer and is calculated as the Sales and Marketing expenses in a given period divided by New Customers acquired in the same period.

CAC Payback Period—The CAC Payback Period is the number of months required to pay back the associated CACs and is calculated as the CAC divided by the Average Monthly Gross Profit.

CAC Ratios—The most common CAC Ratio is defined as the Sales and Marketing expenses divided by the New Subscription Bookings. The Bookings number should be matched with the associated Sales and Marketing expenses to the extent it is a practical exercise. Typically, Enterprise SaaS companies use figures from the same year since variations in the Sales Cycles makes attribution difficult and, usually, not very valuable. Small/Mid-Market SaaS companies typically use the prior quarter or month since the sales cycle is shorter for these businesses. B2C SaaS companies typically use the prior month's Sales and Marketing expenses because the GTM strategy focuses on Call-to-Action marketing, which leads to a quick customer response. The CAC Ratio can be interpreted as the Sales and Marketing investment needed to acquire $1.00 of new Subscription Bookings.

Best practice for SaaS companies is to segment the CAC Ratio into two different ratios according to the type of sales activity defined as New Customer and Expansion. In my experience, the CAC for Expansion Bookings is approximately one-third the cost of acquiring New Customers. Therefore, distinguishing the CAC for each type of sale aids GTM strategy and management. When you use these specific measures, also provide a Blended CAC Ratio, which is the aggregate calculation for the business.

SaaS Magic Numbers and Sales Efficiency

The SaaS Magic Number concept has been around for many years as a representation of Sales Efficiency. Simply put, the Magic Number shows you how much money you earn from spending on acquiring new customers. There are three main approaches to calculating the Magic Number.

The **CLTV/CAC** ratio is the most important. It measures a company's sales efficiency using the relationship between the lifetime value of an average customer and the average cost of acquiring that customer and is a signal of customer profitability and sales and marketing efficiency. A ratio greater than 1.0 implies that the company is generating value on the average new customer acquired. Inversely, a ratio below 1.0 implies that the company is losing value. Investors expect that the CLTV/CAC ratio should be within a range of 0.8–1.3 with a clear path to achieving a ratio above 3.0x. However, the top-performing companies achieve 3.0x–5.0x.

SaaS Magic Number is a ratio of New Subscription Revenue to Sales and Marketing expenses. Put another way, the Magic Number shows how much it costs to acquire $1.00 of Subscription Revenue. Any ratio above 1.0x means that your company generates more New Subscription Bookings than it spends to acquire the customer.

The most accepted formula is to use a ratio of the increase in ARR in the current period to the Sales and Marketing expenses in the prior period. The difference between the two periods should correspond to the length of the sale cycle. This is especially true for high-growth companies, i.e., 3x annual ARR growth. Investors' expectations are that the Magic Number should fall within a narrow range around 1.0x with any ratio above 3.0x indicating a phenomenal operational leverage.

The Magic Number can be used for evaluating public companies with some adjustments. Public companies often do not publish their annual Bookings numbers. Nor do they disclose the ARR at the end of the year, i.e., the Exit ARR. There are two ways in which to apply the Magic Number calculation if you do not have these two figures. Using year-over-year change in ARR, calculated using the Subscription Revenue in the fiscal fourth quarter and multiplying by four, will give a good proxy. As a reminder, the final quarter's numbers will be found in the 10-K for that year, although you may need to subtract the first three quarters from the annual numbers to get to fiscal quarter Subscription Revenue. The second approach is even simpler. You take the year-over-year change in Subscription Revenue and divide it into the Sales and Marketing expenses for the prior year. Be sure to note the method used in your financial reporting.

Sales Efficiency is an adaptation of the Magic Number for Enterprise SaaS companies. Long sales cycles and the variance in time of the sales cycles make defining the "prior period" for Sales and Marketing expenses difficult. Therefore, in such cases, we use the Sales and Marketing expenses in the same period as the New Subscription Bookings, whether actual or forecasted. For example, if you project $20 million in New Subscription Bookings for a given fiscal year, then your Sales and Marketing expenses should, in theory, be ~$20 million to achieve a 1.0x ratio.

Keep in mind that ratios calculated in this manner will be lower than a Magic Number calculation exactly because you are using current period Sales and Marketing expenses.

Key Takeaways

Unit Economics refers to the measurement of the revenues and costs associated with the average customer in a given period, typically a month. It's the most basic view of business performance. You can think of this view as the atomic level; it's indivisible because there's no smaller unit of measurement than a single customer. You will be expected to serve as the expert in Unit Economics.

The CLTV/CAC value of an average customer cohort, with cohort defined as the count of new customers in a given period, is the single best metric for defining a company's performance. If a company can achieve a high CLTV/CAC ratio, then it will require less capital to achieve superior performance. Such companies can choose to fund increased growth, to generate profits, or enhance innovation through investments in Research and Development.

Understanding Unit Economics definitions and the specific figures for your company will position you as a key player in these discussions.

CHAPTER 5

FINANCIAL METRICS

There are several financial metrics used in reporting SaaS company performance. Even though the CFO is the keeper of these metrics, all SaaS operators need to understand them because they describe the financial profile of the company and the company's growth pattern.

Revenue and Gross Margin

Revenue Recognition Date—The date on which the company has met all revenue recognition requirements per GAAP/IFRS as determined by the CFO. This is a change driven by the adoption of ASC 606, which created a new revenue recognition criterion by merging the GAAP and IFRS concepts. Under ASC 606, revenue is recognized when the following criteria are met:

- A customer contract exists

- The contract has identifiable performance obligations

- A transaction price has been determined

- The transaction price has been allocated appropriately

- The performance obligation has been satisfied

Subscription Revenue Gross Margin—The gross profit margin of the subscription software revenue only. Gross Margin is the percentage of revenue remaining after subtracting the direct costs associated with the delivery of the hosted SaaS product in the period the revenues are generated.

Deferred Revenue and Remaining Performance Obligation

After a SaaS customer is active, the company begins to recognize the revenue from the contract with this customer. The revenue that has yet to be earned is a liability to the company and must be accounted for as such. There are two metrics that reflect this liability.

Deferred Revenue—Deferred Revenue, also called Unearned Revenue, is a balance sheet account that represents the liability associated with the delivery of a SaaS product as required by contract. For an individual contract, Deferred Revenue is equal to all of the revenue expected to be recognized over the period defined by the invoice. Enterprise SaaS companies typically require up-front annual payment for new or renewal contracts. On the date an invoice is issued, the SaaS company records the value of the invoice as Deferred Revenue and books the same amount to Accounts Receivable: debit Accounts Receivable and credit Deferred Revenue. When the customer pays the invoice amount, the company credits Accounts Receivable and debits Cash. Receipt of payment does not affect Deferred Revenue. Assuming that the invoice is for an annual term, the company records revenue in each month the revenue is earned. Therefore, the company will debit Deferred Revenue by one-twelfth of the invoice amount and credit Subscription Revenue by the same amount.

On the Balance Sheet, Deferred Revenue is divided into:

- Short-Term Deferred Revenue, which will be recognized within the next twelve months.

- Long-Term Deferred Revenue, which is the amount of revenue expected to be recognized after the next twelve months.

For example, a $360,000 TCV deal with a three-year term and paid up front will generate $120,000 in Short-Term Deferred Revenue and $240,000 in Long-Term Deferred Revenue at date of invoicing. Each month, the company will credit Short-Term Deferred Revenue by $10,000 and debit Subscription Revenue by $10,000. On the one-year anniversary of the invoice date, the company will move the second year of Deferred Revenue into Short-Term Deferred Revenue and continue the monthly revenue recognition cadence for Subscription Revenue.

Remaining Performance Obligation (RPO)—A company's RPO represents the total future performance obligations arising from contractual relationships. More specifically, RPO is the sum of the invoiced amount and the future amounts not yet invoiced for a contract with a customer. The former amount resides on the balance sheet as Deferred Revenue and has always been reported as required by GAAP. The latter obligation, also referred to as Backlog, makes up the non-invoiced amount of the TCV metric. Thus, RPO equals the sum of Deferred Revenue and Backlog. Some public companies have started using a derivative metric, Current Remaining Performance Obligation, or cRPO, which is the sum of Deferred Revenue and Backlog that the company is obligated to deliver over the next twelve months.

Free Cash Flow and the Rule of Forty

In the financial reporting section of the book, we discussed the importance of the Free Cash Flow (FCF) metric as the most appropriate measure of a company's burn rate. Getting FCF correct is also important when calculating the SaaS company's enterprise value.

Free Cash Flow—As a reminder, we define FCF as:

$$\text{Cash flow from operations} +$$
$$\text{Cash flow for investing activities} = \text{Free Cash Flow}$$

The Rule of Forty (RO40)—The RO40 postulates that investors will be willing to pay substantially higher valuations for SaaS companies with combined growth rate and profitability above 40%. The RO40 acts as a yardstick that allows SaaS companies with a wide variety of GTM strategies to benchmark their growth. Some SaaS companies, particularly early-stage companies (typically those with series B or C funding), seek to maximize growth to achieve breakout and dominate their space. Such companies spend heavily to realize the growth required to accomplish these objectives. More mature SaaS companies solidify their market positioning and typically seek to reduce their burn rates through pricing power and increased reliance on efficient upsells and cross-sell strategies. The RO40 also drives your financing strategy. SaaS companies pursuing category creation strategies may need higher levels of Sales and Marketing expenses in the short term in order to achieve growth much later. Those seeking to build complex products may require above-average Research and Development expenses to bring their products to market. Enterprise SaaS companies fall into this category due to long sales cycles and extensive implementation processes. Such companies will perform lower on the RO40 metric.

For the calculation, the growth rate is best measured using the year-over-year comparison of ARR, although Subscription Bookings is a valid approach. Profitability is typically measured using the FCF definition, which is the sum of the company's annual growth rate and the FCF margin. I've seen companies use EBITDA as well. You should choose the metric that best defines your company's profitability.

Theoretical SaaS Financial Profile

With knowledge of Financial Reporting and SaaS metrics, we can now review a theoretical SaaS company financial profile. This example shows the annual results for a SaaS company with $600 million in revenue for this twelve-month period. We can tell that the company is growing because ARR is higher than annual revenue. The reverse would be true if the company had negative growth. Approximately three-quarters of the total revenue is SaaS revenue. The other revenue could come from maintenance and services contracts, one-time professional services for onboarding customers, or a managed services arrangement under which the SaaS company operates the software for the customer. SaaS revenue has a much higher margin than do other revenue sources, so this company has increased gross margin by generating a larger share of its revenue from SaaS.

Operating Expense margins as a percentage of revenue are 25% for Research and Development, 49% for Sales and Marketing, and 12% for General and Administrative. Sales and Marketing typically consumes most of the Operating Expense budget when a company is growing.

This company runs an operating income loss. Backing out depreciation and amortization gets us to Adjusted EBITDA, which is slightly less negative as a percentage of revenue. The company has a high mix of up-front payments, and this can be seen in the positive FCF margin.

Theoretical SaaS Margin Structure	$	% of Revenue
dollars in 000's		
ARR	771,600	n/a
Revenue		
Subscription Revenue	445,600	74%
Other	154,400	26%
Total Revenue	600,000	100%
Cost of Revenue - Subscription	98,032	16%
Cost of Revenue - Professional Services	104,838	17%
Total Cost of Revenue	202,870	34%
Gross Profit	397,130	66%
Gross Margin	66%	
Operating Expense		
Research & Development	150,000	25%
Sales & Marketing	294,000	49%
General & Administrative	72,000	12%
Total Operating Expense	516,000	86%
Operating Income	(118,870)	-20%
Adjusted EBITDA	(85,870)	-14%
Free Cash Flow	39,130	7%

All SaaS companies have a financial reporting profile like this one with the variations mentioned above. Your company's financial reporting should use this exact format so that stakeholders such as investors (both current and potential) and creditors can quickly understand the high-level performance of the business. And the management team should understand this format so that they are prepared to interact with these stakeholders.

Key Takeaways

- Financial metrics connect the operationally oriented Top-Line and Unit Economics to the company's financial reporting relied on by stakeholders, i.e., the board of directors, the CEO and management team, debt lenders, and both current and potential investors. The financial reporting presented in this chapter is universally recognized by these stakeholders who will study these reports and the relevant metrics in great detail. Your mastery of the Top-Line, Unit Economics, and Financial metrics will enable you to best represent the company's performance to stakeholders.

- FCF is the most important financial metric because it's the only one that shows the true amount of cash generated or consumed by the company. Other metrics, such as Operating Income and Adjusted EBITDA do not take into account working capital needs and capital equipment investments and may give a false sense of profitability if shown without FCF.

- We use the RO40 to evaluate SaaS companies with varying strategies. Thus, high-performance companies focused on growth and those focused on profitability should have similar RO40 figures.

- The financial profile of a company is the set of financial metrics and reporting that define the company's current performance and future outlook. The SaaS business model has a specific financial profile, like a fingerprint. A deep understanding of the SaaS financial profile will allow you to quickly evaluate any SaaS company's performance.

CHAPTER 6

USING SAAS METRICS

The Value of Benchmarking

The last two decades of SaaS evolution has generated an enormous amount of information about financial and operational metrics and their reporting. By tapping into this hoard of data, a skilled SaaS professional can create a set of benchmarks from comparable companies (referred to as "comparables") to validate their company's reporting methodology, then use these to drive their annual planning process and evaluate business performance on several levels.

VALIDATE REPORTING METHODOLOGY

Financial reporting methodology varies widely because the SaaS business model is still relatively new. As an example, let's take Gross Margin. In my experience working with Enterprise SaaS companies over the past five years, I've seen a large variance in benchmarks for Gross Margin across subscription software businesses. Using current benchmarks, you'll typically see that the mean Gross Margin for SaaS companies seems to coalesce around the 77% lsevel. However, I've seen actual Gross Margins for SaaS companies ranging from a low of 60% to as high as 95%. Digging into these variances, you discover that the large variance in Gross Margins between SaaS companies is due to different interpretations of direct expenses and costs.

An experienced SaaS professional knows how to use the correct benchmarks, and in this case, those associated with true comparable companies using common definitions of expenses, to assess their company's performance. Comparing your metrics with accurate benchmarking data, you can then validate your reporting methodology and templatize your reporting for stakeholders.

DRIVE THE ANNUAL PLANNING PROCESS

The annual planning process at many SaaS companies often kicks off in midsummer. By then, the CFO should have already distributed planning templates to department heads. The planning process consists of two separate exercises.

TOP-DOWN PLANNING

For the top-down approach to benchmarking, you establish next year's targets for revenue, gross margin, and cash flow. Benchmarking data can provide excellent guidance for establishing next year's targets, answering questions such as:

- How fast does a company like mine grow?

- How much gross profit should we expect?

- What is the Operating Expense we can support under these assumptions?

The answers to these questions for SaaS companies are well documented by widely accepted existing benchmarks. Using data from a wide variety of sources such as the KeyBanc SaaS Survey, the OPEXEngine SaaS benchmarking, Benchsights metrics database, and public comparables, you can guide company CEOs and boards in setting appropriate revenue, gross margin, and cash flow targets.

BOTTOM-UP PLANNING

After completing your top-down planning, you and your management team then develop a bottom-up forecast for expenses.

Benchmarking also provides useful data on spending levels across the major expense categories, e.g., COR and Operating Expense subcategories, Research and Development; Sales and Marketing; and General and Administrative, and specific data on headcount for each team within these categories. For example, you can access Sales headcount data for Account Executives, Sales Development Reps/Business Development Reps, and Renewal Reps along with compensation data. This knowledge gives you the credibility to push back in negotiation around department-level expenses, easing the way toward consensus around a final negotiated solution.

The sum of the cash flow from the top-down exercise and the total expenses from the bottom-up exercise is often negative. In other words, the targeted revenue won't support the level of expenses requested by the management team. Understanding the budget process will allow you to manage the inevitable negotiations around this cash flow gap to land on a final annual plan for the company. This is how you can serve as a trusted business partner to the company.

Operating Margins

Operating Margins are the percentage of revenue metrics for Gross Profit, Operating Expense for Research and Development;

Sales and Marketing; and General and Administrative, Operating Income, and Free Cash Flow. Now that we have nearly two decades of SaaS benchmarks, we know what operating margins should be for a SaaS company, regardless of any unique business dynamics. We use this data to benchmark our margins against those of other companies. Thus, benchmarking data gives your reporting credibility. This is necessary so that you can avoid debates over the reporting and thus engage at a strategic level with stakeholders.

As a specific example from my experience, I started working with a SaaS company in the middle of a significant restructuring. It was clear that we needed to terminate some percentage of the workforce, but the management team could not agree on the post-restructuring headcount. It wasn't until I developed an employee count range based on peer group benchmarks for operating expenses that I was able to gain consensus among company stakeholders for the restructuring.

Go-To-Market (GTM) Strategy

A company's GTM strategy is well established at a high level. SaaS companies with high value, i.e., high ACV, and highly complex software offerings employ expensive field sales teams backed by technical support. Companies that sell lower ACV and less complex products need a more cost-effective sales team using a target mix of outbound and inbound sales. B2C SaaS companies use free-trial and freemium products. All three categories of companies use SaaS metrics, but the type of spending for each category's GTM activities vary greatly. Regardless of a company's GTM strategy, benchmarking data provides guidelines for the sales and marketing spend. For example, a SaaS company with ARR in the $20 million–$40 million range and a year-over-year growth rate in the mid-double digits typically spends about 60%–80% of recognized revenue on sales and marketing, with the mix of sales-to-marketing spend about 75%–25%. Any company in this size range whose spending lies outside of these benchmarks should evaluate their GTM strategy.

Naturally, every company must consider their unique circumstances when using GTM benchmarks. For example, I've worked with several Enterprise SaaS companies with above-average sales and marketing spends. I recall three specific cases in which spending exceeded recognized revenue. All three companies were involved in category creation, i.e., developing and selling software to customers where the customer base did not yet see the need for the product. In these types of category creation plays, companies typically rely on customer evangelism and education to raise awareness of the value proposition, thus increasing the sales and marketing spend beyond comparable benchmarks. The sales cycle is also especially long in such cases and this can also lead to higher sales and marketing spending. Fortunately, the ratio of sales and marketing spending to recognized revenue typically normalizes once companies cross $25 million in ARR.

Key Takeaways

We use benchmarking to:

- Ensure that financial reporting meets those for other SaaS companies, particularly those that are comparable in size and use a similar business strategy.

- Set parameters for the annual planning process. Tying parameters to actual benchmarks adds credibility to your budget and allows you to gain buy-in from management on their department budgets and from the board of directors for your performance forecasts.

- Confirm that your margin reporting is consistent with the standard methodology for the SaaS industry.

- Manage the performance of the company's GTM strategy regardless of target market.

Ultimately, benchmarking overrides opinions gained from non-benchmarking sources and raises the quality of discussions allowing for more time on strategy.

Part 1 Summary

When running a SaaS business, managers must use SaaS metrics and benchmarks to assess operating performance to correctly drive the annual planning process and validate reporting methodology. The results of faster decision making and internal consensus around everything from headcount to gross margin targets will improve operating efficiency while gaining you respect from all stakeholders and enhancing your credibility as a SaaS professional.

Of course, the specific SaaS metrics and benchmarks differ from one SaaS company to the next. As a next step, we will learn two separate classification methodologies for SaaS companies. This knowledge will allow you to best pick the most appropriate SaaS metrics and benchmarks for successful management of your specific business.

PART 2

THE CUSTOMER-CENTRIC SAAS MODEL

The growth of the SaaS industry along with increased complexity of product and service delivery has spawned several subcategories, each of which has its own specific dynamics and metrics. In Part 2, we will review the first of two different types of classification methodologies and discuss how SaaS metrics apply.

I think of the categories as falling along two different axes. The first axis is a customer-centric classification in that SaaS companies are defined by the type of customer they serve. On the second axis, companies are defined by their industry focus. Both classifications provide valuable frameworks for evaluating SaaS companies. The Customer-Centric framework is best suited for management teams who manage their businesses based on the GTM strategy, which is, in turn, based on the customer. The Industry-Centric framework is best suited for investors who seek to understand how the business model can capture value. As an operations-focused CFO, I find the customer-centric classification valuable because it highlights key organization and operational differences that drive strategic decision making.

Customer-Centric Models

As mentioned, using this definition highlights the key operational differences that drive strategic decision making as well as the relevant KPIs for management and reporting.

The three general categories of Customer-Centric models are:

- Enterprise

- SMM (also referred to as Small and Medium Businesses or SMBs)

- B2C

In Part 2, we will review each of these three customer-centric categories in detail, starting with the category definition, moving to the financial profile, GTM strategy, category-specific SaaS metrics, and finishing with an analysis of a representative public company example.

CHAPTER 7

ENTERPRISE SAAS MODEL FINANCIAL PROFILE

Overview

Enterprise SaaS companies serve the largest companies and are defined as those with revenues above $1 billion and employee count above 10,000. We often reference the Fortune 1000 when describing the enterprise customers. These customers demand robust products designed for mission-critical applications for use by hundreds or thousands of their employees. They require high-touch sales engagement and demand high-quality service delivered through both customer support and customer success teams.

Like all SaaS models, Enterprise SaaS companies have high subscription margins, which are currently a median of 78%. However, lower margin professional services revenue accounts for around 20%–40% of total revenue and this reduces the combined gross margin. We define the average ACV range starting at $50,000 and extending into six figures, reflecting the higher costs to develop and deliver the software solution.

Enterprise SaaS companies have specific organization structures designed to meet the demands of serving this customer segment. The GTM strategy requires a *Direct Sales* or *Field Sales* team consisting of Account Executives supported by both sales engineers and Sales Development Representatives (SDRs). Account-Based Marketing is typically the dominant strategy for communicating the value proposition. The professional services organization bears responsibility for implementing the product and enabling the customers' end users to maximize adoption. The customer success organization has a much higher profile and is increasingly led by a vice president or even Chief Experience Officer due to the role this function serves in driving expansion and lower churn.

Typically, the product boasts robust functionality and this often requires extensive integration. To implement the product, the company staffs a strong professional services organization. Implementation time alone can take several months to complete and trigger Go Live. The duration of this time period is known as Time-to-Go Live, the acronym for which is either TTGL or TTL. The time required to get the customer to full adoption, known as Time-to-Value (TTV) will take even longer.

Financial Profile

There are a number of unique aspects to the Enterprise SaaS business model. The time required to onboard new customers—product integration and implementation—means special attention must be given to revenue recognition. The GTM emphasis on Direct Sales means that total Sales and Marketing expenses weigh toward Sales, and this requires specific Financial Planning and Analysis reporting. The need for Professional Services leads to lower consolidated Gross Margins than in other types of SaaS companies. Enterprise SaaS companies build robust Customer Success organizations as part of the customer retention strategy, thereby increasing Sales expenses. Marketing investment is used in Account-Based Marketing, a strategy unique to Enterprise SaaS companies. Finally, nearly all contracts will have annual terms which require annual up-front payments, and this greatly enhances FCF. As such, it is important to remember that Operating Income is not a proxy for cash flow.

Revenue Recognition

Typically, the main challenge for Enterprise SaaS revenue recognition is in determining the point at which the company meets the performance obligation. I've seen a wide variety of methods used to determine when a company satisfies a performance obligation. On one end of the spectrum, companies begin recognizing revenue when the customer signs off on the implementation, therefore triggering a Go Live event. A more conservative approach is the use of the TLV date, which can be the point at which all training and enablement has been completed or the point at which all licenses (seats) are actively used.

The period of time between the Bookings Date and the Revenue Recognition Date creates unusual fluctuations in the Subscription Revenue line item. At the Bookings Date, accounting records the annual contract with a journal entry that debits Accounts Receivable and credits Deferred Revenue with Deferred Revenue to be debited monthly over the period of the contract converting it to revenue. Since we must wait a period of time for the revenue recognition, accounting will book a Deferred Revenue "catch-up," which converts the months since Bookings Date to revenue in a single period. As a result, Subscription Revenue will vary significantly from period to period. You will find that reporting Annual Recurring Revenue (ARR) off one period's Monthly Recurring Revenue (MRR) will not be valuable in this case. This is the reason we use Contracted Annual Recurring Revenue (CARR) in place of ARR.

Gross Margin

Accountants often say that establishing revenue recognition in accordance with ASC 606 is the most difficult process to implement, but in my experience, producing a policy for gross margin accounting is much more challenging because there is not an established set of rules to follow, only concepts.

Conducting your gross margin analysis will draw on several accounting, legal, and financial concepts.

Direct Costs—Direct costs refer to expenses associated with delivery of the SaaS offering or services. You can also think about direct and indirect costs as the expenses associated with the activities that the customer consumes in an accounting period, such as the right to use the software and on-demand customer support. For financial reporting, direct costs are classified as COR.

Indirect Costs—Indirect costs are expenses associated with the functions required to run the business organization. You can also think about indirect costs as the expenses associated with the activities that customers do not consume. For financial reporting, indirect costs are classified as Operating Expense. We separate direct and indirect costs to allow for better understanding of the production costs and margins.

Matching Principle—The third concept is the "matching" principle, which requires companies to report expenses on its income statement in the period in which the related revenues are earned rather than activities that add value to the customer in future periods.

Customer Obligation—Your customer Service Level Agreement, or SLA, establishes the contractual obligation to provide the support activities offered. For example, you may offer customers live support twenty-four hours a day, seven days a week. To meet this obligation, you will need to staff a team to be on call for inbound customer requests.

Benchmarking—It is important to compare your recommended gross margin with that of comparable companies. Any gross margin result outside of the norm is a sign that you should review your analysis more closely.

Cost of Revenue "Buckets"

For Enterprise SaaS models, direct costs are those activities associated with the delivery of the hosted software. There are four main types.

1. HOSTING AND INFRASTRUCTURE EXPENSES

Subscription software requires a hosting environment that includes:

- Servers for processing and storage

- Internet connectivity

- Software that provides security, control, and monitoring services

This is also referred to as the cloud environment.

Your business can manage its own hosting environment internally, but venture-backed companies will use a third-party provider such as Amazon Web Services (AWS), Microsoft Azure, or Google Cloud, among a host of others. According to the 2019 KeyBanc Capital Markets SaaS Survey, which focuses on venture-backed companies, only 12% of surveyed companies operate internal hosting environments.

What makes accounting for third-party Hosting and Infrastructure costs difficult is that your company uses Hosting and Infrastructure for specific use cases. These include revenue generation obviously, but for Research and Development and Sales and Marketing as well.

REVENUE GENERATION: DIRECT COST

The first use case is revenue generation—running the software for the customer. Companies use a production environment for service delivery, i.e., hosting, bandwidth, and storage for all paid customer activity in a given accounting period. The revenue generated from those customers in that period is associated with a direct cost to be booked as COR.

SOFTWARE DEVELOPMENT AND TESTING: INDIRECT COST

A second use case for Hosting and Infrastructure is for software development and testing. SaaS companies maintain a development environment, which is completely separate from the production environment. Engineers use this environment to expand the capabilities of the software running in the production environment. This innovation cost is not required for the current service delivery process. We do expect that this activity will add value to customers in future periods as software updates are put into revenue production. Therefore, expenses associated with this activity are indirect and should be recorded in Operating Expense under Research and Development.

FREE TRIALS AND FREEMIUM PRODUCTS: INDIRECT COST

A third use case is related to Sales and Marketing. Some companies offer free trials or freemium products as part of their GTM strategy. Marketing investment drives free trial or freemium users, and the company uses additional marketing and inside sales representatives to convert these users to paid subscribers.

Box, Inc. provides us with a good example of a free trial offering. The SaaS cloud content management provider offers a fourteen-day free trial to generate leads. Marketing drives potential users to the free trial landing page with a self-service provisioning option. Box then uses email marketing and inside sales representatives who reach out to the free users to convert them into paid subscribers. Data center and customer support costs related to serving these free users are booked to Sales and Marketing.

Web performance and security company Cloudflare, Inc. provides a good example of a freemium product offering. Cloudflare also accounts for the hosting and infrastructure costs associated with free users in Sales and Marketing. In my estimation, Cloudflare's free users cost the company 1.6%–2.5% of total revenue. The marketing investment and the free-to-paid conversion rate of these users drive the ROI of this GTM strategy.

As CFO, you will need to allocate the amount of the third-party hosting and infrastructure invoice between direct and indirect costs per the specific use case.

COLOCATION EXPENSES: DIRECT COST

Larger companies own and operate their own hosting facilities. Doing so is a complex activity but offers greater control over cloud operations and is usually less expensive at the scale at which these companies operate. Internal hosting operations require additional skillsets. On-site workers maintain the servers, provide security, and run the building maintenance. The company pays directly for the significant amount of energy needed to run the servers as well as networking and interconnection fees. The servers and networking equipment are purchased, requiring the booking of depreciation expenses. If the company leases all or a portion of the building, i.e., colocation expenses, then these expenses should be recorded as Assets and Liabilities.

PROPRIETARY SOFTWARE: DIRECT COST

Whether the cloud is hosted internally or externally, companies will likely have built proprietary software required to run the company's platform. Software developed internally should be recorded as an Asset and amortized when this software is placed into production. Subsequent updates will add to amortization schedules when placed into production. The amortization expenses should be included in the "Hosting and Infrastructure" category. I would like to point out that the process of tracking developer hours is a complicated endeavor. Many companies choose to expense software development because the administrative workload of managing developer hours is too high.

THIRD-PARTY SOFTWARE: DIRECT COST

Companies also employ third-party software for monitoring performance, which is typically referred to as Application Performance Monitoring (APM) and includes providers such as AppDynamics (Cisco), Datadog APM and Distributed Tracking, Microsoft Application Insights, New Relic APM, Splunk Enterprise and IT Service Intelligence, and Stackify Retrace, among many others. Many companies purchase data feeds and make the data accessible to the customer as part of the software offering. These types of software directly support your customer solution and should be classified as COR.

2. CUSTOMER SUPPORT VERSUS CUSTOMER SUCCESS

Customer support is the most widely misinterpreted item because two internal departments—**Customer Support and Customer Success**—focus on customers, and both have Customer in their names. The former is always a direct cost; the latter's role in serving customers must be closely evaluated.

CUSTOMER SUPPORT: DIRECT COST

Customer Support is the on-demand support offering technical assistance. These services will be included in the customer contract, meaning that you need to adequately staff the customer support team to ensure customers can effectively engage with your software. This means that the expenses required to maintain an on-demand customer support team should be included in COR regardless of the customer activity volume.

Typical customer calls are related to access issues ("My password doesn't work"), feature usage ("How do I launch a campaign?"), and bug reporting ("A hyperlink doesn't work"). These employee costs are direct since they provide value to the customer in the same period as that of the service.

The customer support team will field questions that require a higher level of technical knowledge. Often, employees from Customer Success and even Research and Development will be called on to help. However, this does not mean that associated employee expenses related to these functions should be included in the COR. If you find that these activities have a low frequency or involve work that crosses several accounting periods, then you should leave these expenses in the Operating Expense category.

However, if your software has significant product gaps that require technical skill for customers to use it, then you probably have engineers engaged in customer work on a routine basis. In this case, you should define and classify the associated expenses as COR.

Customer support will also require software tools that facilitate communication and support ticket tracking, and these software and systems expenses should be included as well. Popular software tools include Zoho Desk, HubSpot, LiveAgent, Freshdesk, Zendesk, Groove, and Help Scout.

Customer Support payroll and associated expenses should be classified in COR as well because this activity directly supports the product in the period revenue is earned from the product. Additionally, customer support is likely required to be provided by the customer contract, and this adds further evidence for recording as COR.

CUSTOMER SUCCESS: INDIRECT COST

The Customer Success department's mission is completely different from that of customer support. Customer Success provides services that benefit the company by maximizing the value add that your software delivers to your customers. Key objectives are to increase customer engagement to ensure that your value add matches the customers' expectations at the close of the original sale. You will want to ensure that your customers make use of all the services they purchased. If you price your service on a per-seat basis, you will want to maximize the number of seat licenses that are in active use. If you use a tiered volume pricing model, you will want your customers to use all the capacity they purchased. In addition, you will want to connect with the end users, who are your customers' employees or customers, to ensure they fully understand and use all the features available.

Customer Success activities do not generate revenue in the period when customer success activities were performed. Instead, these activities increase the probability of renewal and/or expansion in future periods by maximizing your customers' satisfaction with your product. Therefore, it is an indirect cost, which is an operating cost.

The Customer Success department also plays a key role in defining the product roadmap. The Customer Success team's activities provide it with the best understanding of customer metrics and, therefore, customer behavior. They see firsthand which features and functionality work and which ones do not. They understand which specific use cases work best and which frustrate or annoy your customers. The knowledge they build is invaluable to the product marketing, product development, and engineering teams, which will incorporate this knowledge into the product roadmap. In fact, the best performing organizations hold weekly collaboration meetings between the Customer Success and Research and Development teams to support continual adjustments to the product functionality. One should think of Research and Development expenses as an investment in future revenue; therefore, associated costs for all activities that drive innovation are indirect and should be included in Operating Expense. Customer Success expenses should be classified as an Operating Expense because it supports revenue indirectly, i.e., it drives customer engagement over several periods and it helps to inform the product roadmap for future software development.

Customer Success teams use many of the same software tools listed in the Customer Support section. There are Customer Success-specific tools available as well. Of these, my personal favorite is Totango, but I also like Monday, Capacity, and AgileCRM. Smaller companies may want to evaluate Krow, a lower-cost Customer Success engine.

CUSTOMER SUPPORT/CUSTOMER SUCCESS HYBRID MODELS
Many companies, especially those in the early stages, use a single team of people responsible for both customer support and customer success. Even more complicating is that your engineers

may field customer inquiries as part of their job responsibilities. Basically, these folks pick up the phone anytime customers call. If this is the case in your company, you will want to allocate associated expenses between COR and Operating using estimates of time spent on customer-facing work.

3. CLOUD OPERATIONS AND PLATFORM SUPPORT EXPENSES

In general, companies classify expenses associated with platform operations as COR since these activities maintain the operational efficiency of the hosted software for revenue recognition in the same period. Companies increasingly staff cybersecurity experts to manage cloud operational security, and these expenses are direct.

Many companies have third-party fees such as transaction expenses and external data. Transaction fees are the direct result of a customer activity and should be treated as direct expenses. If your business takes credit cards, then you should account for payment processing fees in COR. Square, Stripe, Clover, and PayPal, among many others, are examples of payment processors, the fees for which should be included in the COR.

Some companies use patented software to support their proprietary software. For example, leading public cloud infrastructure providers and e-commerce platforms, such as Heroku and Amazon Web Services, use Twilio's SendGrid digital communication platform, and these expenses are incorporated into COR. Zendesk and HubSpot use Cloudflare's Content Distribution Network (CDN) for service delivery and include those associated expenses in COR.

External data used in the software are direct if needed to provide the software with the full functionality as marketed to the consumer. A cybersecurity leader, Kenna Security, now part of Cisco, uses third-party subscription data feeds for threat intelligence assessment and records these fees as COR.

PROFESSIONAL SERVICES EXPENSE

All Professional Services activities are direct expenses. However, utilization of the team members will never be 100% focused on customer activities, mainly because it is difficult to match demand for services with supply of services. The Professional Services leadership tracks the sales pipeline and financial forecasts and staffs the team accordingly but will never match supply and demand. Therefore, the percentage of the team's time focused on internal activities unrelated to customers should remain in Sales and Marketing, while time focused on customers should be allocated to COR. Employee expenses must be reported on a fully loaded basis, i.e., with all compensation-related expenses such as payroll taxes, benefits, bonuses, and stock-based compensation. Finally, most companies allocate overhead, such as applicable shared rent and utilities, to COR based on relative headcount. Overhead allocations are incorporated into line items associated with the salaries and wages in this case.

Free Cash Flow

In every client engagement, I strongly encourage companies to use up-front payments as a means of improving their cash flow. I get pushback from product and sales teams, both of whom believe that customers will only accept monthly payments. Having managed the software budget process in a Fortune 500 company, I know for a fact that enterprise customers *only* buy software on annual contracts with up-front payments. Plus, the value of up-front payments to the company's working capital position is so powerful that SaaS companies ultimately move to this approach.

Up-front payments have always been standard at perpetual software companies. Customers purchased the rights to use software in perpetuity, and this generated the cash necessary for software vendors to achieve an immediate ROI for software development and customer acquisition. With the rise of SaaS companies, one of the benefits touted for customers was that they could spread payments over future months. SaaS companies soon realized the devastating impact to their working capital because it took several periods for the customer's payments to cover the customer acquisition costs and longer to cover software development costs. Companies quickly moved to up-front payments.

A comparison between annual and monthly payments illustrates the different impacts on working capital for an Enterprise SaaS business model. We'll use the investment in customer acquisition only. It's not that we ignore the Research and Development cost; we set the ROI metric high enough to ensure we can support these activities. This approach relies on the CLTV/CAC metric because if we can achieve a high enough ratio, then we can earn enough from customers to cover Research and Development expenses as well as that of General and Administrative expenses. A CLTV/CAC ratio of 3x ensures that we can cover these expenses.

The chart below shows the impact of an up-front payment compared to monthly payments for a twelve-month contract with an ACV of $75,000 and showing the payback on the investment in acquiring a single customer. Starting with a CLTV/CAC ratio of 3x and assuming a 78% gross margin and eighteen-month Customer Lifetime, we can calculate CAC as such:

$75,000 ACV × 80% Gross Margin ×
1.5 year Customer Lifetime Value = $90,000

$90,000 / 3x CLTV/CAC ratio = $30,000

Upfront payments significantly improve working capital, driving positive cash flow in period 1 versus period 5 in our example.

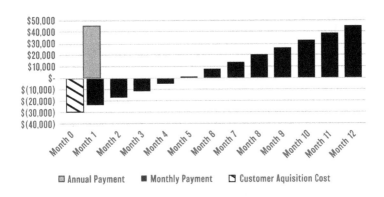

Impact of Annual Upfront Payments - Cumulative Cash Flows
for Annual and Monthly Payments

■ Annual Payment   ■ Monthly Payment   ◻ Customer Aquisition Cost

Starting with this ACV, we calculate the optimum CAC by applying assumptions for a gross margin and a customer lifetime to the ACV and dividing the product by a best-in-class CLTV/CAC ratio of 3.0x. The calculation is ACV x 78% gross margin x 1.5 years divided by 3.0x for a CAC of approximately $30,000. Under these assumptions, cash flow break-even is achieved in the first month with an upfront annual payment versus breakeven at five months with monthly payments.

Using these assumptions, the company achieves breakeven (and then some) in one month with an annual up-front payment but will need five months to do so with monthly payments.

Up-front payments also require a different look at the financials. When reviewing the financials, it is important to remember that the operating income is not a proxy for cash flow. Instead, Bookings and Billings activity drive cash flow. Therefore, it is important to see the financial plan with the profit and loss statement, balance sheet, *and* cash flow statement.

The final point here is that the Enterprise SaaS working capital surplus increases with the growth rate: the faster the companies grow, the greater their cash flow from operations. Of course, this dynamic is a double-edged sword in that declining revenue growth will increase the need for cash. And a negative-growth company will find new financing challenging.

Theoretical Financial Profile

Using the information above, we can assemble a theoretical Enterprise SaaS model for the first five years starting with the first year of sales. In doing so, we revisit the same exercise in Part 1 but with more detail.

First, we'll start with ARR growth, which is modeled on the T2D3 concept. Colloquially, the term "T2D3" refers to a growth trajectory of two years of tripling revenue followed by three years of doubling revenue from a starting point in the mid-single-dollar millions. It is not a theoretical concept but is based on an analysis of the growth trajectories of the highest growth technology companies since the turn of the century. More specifically, it represents the median growth trajectory of this rare cohort and shows what is possible—an aspirational target that very few can achieve. We use this concept to serve as the upper range for our revenue forecast and discount it based on our historical performance and future investments. For our theoretical financial profile, we will use the T2D3 concept for the growth trajectory.

Our exercise will also include these assumptions:

- Initially, New Bookings convert into ARR following a two-month implementation cycle.

- New ARR is added consistently over the twelve-month period and converts to revenue monthly (ignoring seasonality for the sake of simplicity).

- Subscription Revenue is amortized monthly over twelve months and will always lag ARR as a result. The variance will shrink by a diminishing margin as the company grows its ARR base.

- The company's ability to monetize Professional Services is limited, as shown by low revenue and high direct costs in the early years, but grows quickly with experience and implementation toolkits.

- Operating Expense grows with the company, but the ratios of Research and Development, Sales and Marketing, and General and Administrative to Total Operating Expense stay nearly constant at 0.3, 0.5, and 0.2, respectively.

- Sales expenses consistently make up 70% of the Sales and Marketing budget.

- Sales Efficiency stays above 1.0x at this growth rate, representing perfect execution.

- FCF benefits from up-front annual payments adjusted downward for collections delay.

- Non-Recurring Bookings are assumed to be collected in the same period (for simplicity).

This is a purely theoretical exercise showing an Enterprise SaaS company with high growth and perfect operational execution, but it is based on my CFO experience as well as my research on these types of business models. Understanding this theoretical financial profile will give you the basis for evaluating Enterprise SaaS companies.

Theoretical Enterprise Saas Margin Structure	Year 1	Year 2	Year 3	Year4	Year 5
Subscription Bookings	$ 1,200	$ 2,400	$ 7,200	$ 10,800	$ 21,600
New ARR	1,000	2,200	6,400	10,200	19,800
CARR	1,200	3,600	10,800	21,600	43,200
ARR	1,000	3,200	9,600	19,800	39,600
Revenue					
Subscription Revenue	458	2,108	6,333	14,850	29,775
Professional Services Revenue	240	480	5,040	7,560	15,120
Total Revenue	698	2,588	11,373	22,410	44,895
Cost of Revenue - Subscription	138	590	1,457	3,416	6,551
Cost of Revenue - Professional	228	422	3,326	4,838	9,072
Total Cost of Revenue	366	1,013	4,783	8,254	15,623
Gross Profit	333	1,576	6,590	14,156	29,273
Gross Margin	48%	61%	58%	63%	65%
Operating Expense					
Research & Development	279	984	3,412	6,051	11,224
Sales & Marketing	670	1,631	6,938	11,205	21,999
General & Administrative	140	440	1,706	2,913	5,387
Total Operating Expense	1,089	3,054	12,056	20,169	38,610
Operating Income	(757)	(1,479)	(5,465)	(6,013)	(9,337)
Free Cash Flow	(255)	(467)	(2,439)	(1,423)	(232)
Margin Structure					
Gross Margin - Subscription	70%	72%	77%	77%	78%
Gross Margin - PS	5%	12%	34%	36%	40%
Research & Development	40%	38%	30%	27%	25%
Sales & Marketing - Sales	66%	44%	43%	36%	35%
Sales & Marketing - Marketing	30%	19%	18%	14%	14%
Total Sales & Marketing	96%	63%	61%	50%	49%
General & Administrative	20%	17%	15%	13%	12%
Total Operating Expense	156%	118%	106%	90%	86%
Free Cash Flow	-37%	-18%	-21%	-6%	-1%

Key Takeaways

To summarize, the Enterprise SaaS financial profile is unique in many ways:

- Bookings to ARR—The time it takes to onboard a new customer due to implementation, systems integration, and training activities creates a timing difference between the date of Bookings and the date of revenue recognition. Reporting both CARR and ARR resolves this timing issue.

- Sales and Marketing—The high-value product requires an expensive Direct Sales GTM strategy and light touch marketing strategies supported by a strong leadership team and effective support infrastructure.

- FCF—Operating Income is not a proxy for FCF because all contracts require up-front payments. Whereas Subscription Revenue is amortized over twelve months, the Bookings amount is collected up front.

Understanding the theoretical financial profile of an Enterprise SaaS company gives you a basis for understanding best-in-class performance. You can use this benchmark to plan the upper limit of revenue and profitability for the budget process. In my work, I like to start the annual budget process by presenting this theoretical framework to expand the management team's idea of what is possible.

CHAPTER 8

ENTERPRISE GO-TO-MARKET STRATEGY

The Enterprise SaaS GTM strategy leads with Direct Sales and the supporting team and requires heavy professional services and customer success teams. A key component of the financial modeling and performance tracking revolves around Sales Capacity Planning, which illustrates the financial connection between the Direct Sales team budget and New Bookings. Enterprise SaaS companies also use partnerships to sell products when doing so would not otherwise be cost efficient.

Organization

The entire budget for the GTM strategy will be accounted for in the Sales and Marketing category, which includes the Sales, Customer Success (unless allocated as described earlier), Business Development, and Marketing departments.

DIRECT SALES

The Direct Sales team is supported by a team of folks who work new opportunities, manage the administrative tasks, and provide leadership.

The Sales Operation team manages the front end of the Quote-To-Cash process by providing product quotes, supporting legal contract work, and recording the performance of the entire GTM strategy.

The Chief Revenue Officer leads the sales team and typically oversees sales managers, who, in turn, directly manage the Account Executives (AEs) and Sales Development Representatives. The Sales Development Representatives respond to leads generated by marketing campaigns and nurture these opportunities until the stage where they can be passed to AEs.

There are several different types of sales representatives:

Account Executive—The AE is the key customer-facing member of the Direct Sales team, responsible for closing deals to create new customers. AEs earn a base salary and a commission on sales of the company's product. The sales commission compensation is designed to generate 50% of the AE's total earnings if the AE meets a specific sales target, called a quota. The Sales Quota is almost always an annual target. If the AE exactly meets the Sales Quota, then the total earnings are referred to as On-Target-Earnings, or OTE. At OTE, 50% of the total compensation comes from salary and 50% from sales commission. The OTE is a key metric because the annual quota is set at a multiple of four to six times OTE. The exact number will vary on several factors including the company's growth stage, the sales cycle length, and the ACV. This ratio is important because it drives the main cost component in sales and marketing.

Enterprise SaaS companies build complex products and sell into large corporations. The sales process requires building relationships with key decision makers inside the organization, developing an understanding of the organization's technology needs, educating the organization on the value add of the product, advising the organization on the integration and implementation, and getting the organization to purchase the product. This period is known as the Sales Cycle. Managing the Sales Cycle requires a senior sales representative with two to five years of quota-carrying sales experience plus another two to four years of entry-level sales experience.

Inside Sales Representative (ISR)—The term "Inside Sales" used to refer to the process of closing deals remotely without the live, face-to-face engagement of the direct sales approach. The onset of the pandemic made all selling remote, so this is no longer an accurate distinction. Today, the better definition is to describe Inside Sales as the use of lower cost sales strategy leveraging people who do not need the selling skills of AEs combined with a robust digital marketing lead-generation program. The marketing campaigns generate contact information of potential customers who demonstrate interest through some behavior such as attending a webinar or responding to a call-to-action message. The objective of these marketing campaigns is to increase brand awareness and further customer education to move respondents closer to a sale. The ISR then reaches out to each interested customer and attempts to move them to a paid subscription. The Inside Sales strategy is successful if the combination of the digital marketing campaigns and the ISR results in greater sales efficiency than either a Direct Sales or an all-digital marketing strategy.

The ISR's work is far more predictable and regulated than that of an AE. Each day, the ISR has a set of targets to accomplish. These include sending emails and making phone calls to potential customers on contact lists. And it's more difficult to tie these activities directly to sales. So each month, the ISR is measured on opportunities created and opportunities converted to paying customers. Variable compensation is often based on meeting daily and month activity targets and sometimes in lieu of commission on new deals.

Sales Development Representative (SDR)—SDRs support AEs by prospecting for Sales Opportunities and nurturing these leads to the point where AEs can work with them on closing the deal. This activity can be outbound in that the SDR directly contacts decision makers for potential customers by phone or email. Or it can be an inbound activity in that the SDR responds to emails or phone calls from prospective customers. At the point of contact, the SDR seeks to determine if the potential customers' software needs fit the company's software product. If there is a match, then the SDR will pass the lead to the AE.

Business Development Representative (BDR)—In larger organizations, the SDR job transitions into separate roles that manage inbound and outbound activities. The SDR will focus exclusively on qualifying inbound leads in support of the AEs. The BDR assumes the role of outbound activities and leverages emails, phone calls, and social selling tools to add Sales Opportunities in the pipeline. The BDR compensation is similar to that of an SDR.

PROFESSIONAL SERVICES

The Professional Services team manages the onboarding of new customers. This function includes project management, systems integration, and training. Nearly all of these expenses are related to the team members, either employees or contractors. Early-stage companies often provide these services for free, and this drags down gross margin, sometimes to a negative rate. More mature companies can bill for services rendered, and this revenue generates a 40% gross margin as is typical for all services firms.

CUSTOMER SUCCESS

The Customer Success team manages the customer relationship to ensure satisfaction with the SaaS offering, thus ensuring the contract renewal. Additionally, the team seeks to drive opportunities for expansion of the existing contract. In mature companies, the Customer Success team often owns the responsibility for Renewal and Expansion Bookings and are commissioned on these deals.

MARKETING

About 30% of the Sales and Marketing expenses are dedicated to marketing. The most popular approach in Enterprise SaaS marketing is a strategy referred to as **Account-Based Marketing** or ABM. In an ABM strategy, the company markets to key business accounts directly rather than a one-to-many approach used in Digital Marketing. Marketers identify high-value accounts and key stakeholders within these accounts and then develop marketing campaigns tailored to these key stakeholders and execute through channels distinct to these folks. SDRs nurture the leads and pass them to AEs.

Sales Capacity Planning

Sales Capacity Planning is a modeling exercise conducted to forecast the amount of bookings—New, Expansion, and Renewals—that the sales organization can achieve. This exercise is referred to as the Bookings Build in that we start with assumptions of the sales force productivity and build a Bookings forecast for the year. The Bookings Build is a key analysis in the company's annual budgeting process, financial forecasting, and Sales Incentive Plan development.

For Direct Sales, the expected annual production is forecast using a Sales Capacity Plan. The output is a function of:

- The number of quota-carrying sales representatives (e.g., AEs)

- Their Quota expressed in ACV for both subscription and non-recurring revenue such as professional services

- Their Productivity, expressed as a percentage of total expected annual production

The Productivity factor is a conservative assumption we use to account for lower-than-expected Bookings that takes into account the likely variability in performance among AEs. The term "Over-Assignment Factor" is sometimes substituted for Productivity (except that the terms are the inverse of each other). Over-Assignment Factor is also used to increase quota targets as a way to provide a buffer to lower productivity more than what was modeled.

Adjustments are made for AEs with shorter tenures and, therefore, are still ramping, i.e., Ramping AEs. Typical ramp time is nine months, with a percentage of fully ramped production estimated at each subsequent month. For example, although new AEs may have no production in the first quarter after their start date, they begin to generate small volume in their second quarter of employment (and this could be 25% of total quota) and ramp to 75% of annual quota in their third quarter. In their fourth quarter of employment, these AEs will be responsible for their full quota. Additionally, you should adjust for seasonality if your business experiences it.

Sales Incentive Plan

The sales representatives employed in a Direct Sales GTM strategy have unique compensation structures in that half of the total compensation is based on their sales production. Using a Direct Sales team is expensive, so it makes sense to tie compensation to production.

A Sales Incentive Plan should be a simple and straightforward document that allows sales representatives to easily understand how they can earn sales commissions and at rates that provide incentive to produce the required Bookings as defined by the annual operating plan or budget.

Under a Sales Incentive Plan, each sales representative has a base salary and a variable commission target, called a Target Incentive Commission (TIC) or On-Target-Incentive (OTI). The base and variable amounts are typically split 50%-50%, meaning that the sales representative can earn twice their base salary by producing enough Bookings to hit a contractual target, known as a quota. The sum of the base and variable compensation is known as On-Target-Earnings or OTE. If a sales representative meets their assigned quota, then they will earn 100% of their OTE. Sales representatives who are assigned a quota are called Quota-Carrying Reps or QCRs.

To achieve their variable compensation, QCRs receive a predetermined, contractual percentage of the dollar value of the sale. The value of the sale is always expressed in annual terms, e.g., the ACV. The commission rate is based on the value of the bookings type. For example, higher margin Subscription Bookings carry a higher commission rate than that for Services. Further, QCRs earn a higher commission rate on New Bookings than they do on Expansion Bookings because the latter is already a customer with a known propensity to purchase the product. The Sales Cycle is typically much shorter and requires much less time than does a New Booking. Similarly, Renewal Bookings pay an even lower rate than both New and Expansion Bookings.

The percentage of the Bookings ACV paid to the sales representative is called the Base Commission Rate or BCR and they vary as follows:

- New Bookings: 10% of ACV

- Expansion Bookings: 8% of ACV

- Renewal Bookings: 3% of ACV

- Services: 2% of Contract Value

Companies further incentivize QCRs by offering incremental commission rates once the QCRs meet their quotas using what is called an Accelerator Plan. The plan accelerates sales commissions for Subscription Bookings with incremental rates at various stages over 100% of quota. A typical Accelerator Plan uses a schedule as follows:

- 100% to 125% = 3%

- 125%+ to 150% = 4%

- 150%+ to 200% = 5%

- 200%+ to 250% = 6%

- 250%+ = resets to original commission rate

To illustrate, a QCR who has already met their quota in a given year and closes a New Subscription Booking that increases total annual production to 120% will be commissioned at a rate

3% higher than the 10% BCR, or 13%. This incremental commission rate steps up in stages until a certain point when the rate drops back down to the BCR. This reset protects the company from paying an outsized commission rate on a deal that likely requires support from across the organization, including executives.

Although we focused on QCRs, other members of the sales team have compensation plans with a variable component based on Bookings production by the QCRs. Even though these folks do not personally generate Bookings, they have a significant impact on the QCRs' ability to do so. Sales leadership will receive commissions based on the production of their direct reports, as will middle managers such as those who manage QCRs in their GTM scope, i.e., specific geographies or market verticals. The sales operations team and other supporting members may have variable components in their compensation plan. And the Sales Incentive Plan will provide details for all of these teams.

These incremental expenses are typically shown as a rate which is known as the Fully Loaded Sales Commission Rate, or simply "Loading." Generally speaking, these overhead expenses add 6% to the BCR. For example, a $120,000 ACV New Subscription Booking will pay 10% to the QCR and 6% to the team members qualified for a commission. When modeling sales commission expenses, make sure that you calculate the Fully Loaded Sales Commission Expense.

Sales Commission Expense

So, what is a good target for sales commission expenses as a percentage of revenue? Benchmarks are hard to find because it's not a widely available metric and because the percentage varies significantly from one company to another. So let's create a theoretical company and estimate this metric based on standard commission rates. Assume an Enterprise SaaS company that generated $150 million in total annual revenue with:

- $120 million ARR on annual contacts

- $20 million in service revenue

- 90% gross retention rate

- 120% net retention rate

- 40% growth in the most recent fiscal year

Using these assumptions, we know that the company:

- Started the year with $86 million in ARR

- Renewed $77 million in ARR

- Lost $9 million due to churn and contraction

- Generated Expansion Bookings of $26 million

- Added $17 million in New Bookings

- Grew ARR to $120 million

The sales team also sold $30 million in Services Bookings. Total sales commission expenses would equal $9.3 million or 6.2% of total revenue as follows:

- New Bookings: 10% of $17 million in New ARR equals $1.7 million in commission expenses

- Expansion Bookings: 8% of $26 million in Expansion ARR equals $2.1 million in commission expenses

- Renewal Bookings: 3% of $77 million in Renewal ARR equals $2.3 million in commission expenses

- Services: 2% of Contract Value of $30 million equals $0.6 million in commission expenses

- Loading is an incremental 6% of total sales commission expenses for New and Expansion Subscription Bookings or $2.6 million

We can take this theoretical analysis a bit further to show that sales commission expenses would be about one-fifth of the total sales department expenses. To do this, we assume that this company operates at the RO40, meaning that the EBITDA margin is 0%. Median Gross Margin should be approximately 78%, and Sales and Marketing expenses would be about half of the operating expenses, so $60 million. Sales alone would make up 70% of this amount or $41 million. Therefore, sales commission expenses of $9.2 million would be 22% of the total investment in Sales.

Partnerships

Many SaaS companies use channel partnerships as a way to sell into organizations or markets that the company itself cannot access efficiently. For example, selling to government organizations requires a very specific understanding of the federal, state, and local government procurement process and the associated technology requirements, especially those concerning security and stability. Large prospective customers, such as Fortune 500 corporations, will require specific technology review, procurement processes, and extensive pre-sales support as well as thorough knowledge of the employees involved in the purchasing decision. Sales to highly regulated industry verticals such as financial institutions and healthcare organizations requires knowledge of specific regulations. In some cases, a company has built an extensive network in a certain industry vertical and understands the pain points and use cases specific to that vertical. And, of course, companies seek local partners in countries where they do not have a presence and where sales volume does not justify creating a subsidiary there. Partnering with such an organization can accelerate the sales cycle, lowering the CAC even with channel fees on new business.

Partnership strategy execution requires a dedicated internal organization that sources, vets, onboards, and manages the partnership. Headed by a VP or higher-level executive, the Business Development or Strategic Partnership team will consist of Channel Sales Account Managers or Channel Sales Representatives who manage the day-to-day relationship. A variable compensation is typically based on partnership activity such as leads generated rather than on the ACV of the paid subscriber, although there may be a commission plan for the sales team. The partner is paid a referral fee structured as a percentage of the ACV or on a fee per lead generated. SaaS companies must take into account the full expenses of the partnership activities when calculating CLTV/CAC for this strategy.

As a GTM strategy, developing Strategic Partnerships with other companies can make a huge impact in lowering CACs and in achieving scale earlier in the company's life cycle.

Enterprise SaaS companies typically rely on two categories of partnership opportunities.

CO-SELLING PARTNERSHIPS

In Co-Selling Partnerships, two companies with distinct software products agree to collaborate on their GTM strategies in targeting the same customers. The specific products have differing functionality but both offer value to the same customer. The Direct Sales teams from each company generate and share Sales Opportunities. The level of cooperation will obviously vary in practice. The dynamics vary directly with the relative power of each partner. Take, for example, two partners with similar reputations, i.e., brand awareness, credibility, and quality, and with products of similar value added. This is the formula for an equal partnership. Direct Sales team members meet with potential customers together and collaborate on contracts. Each partner signs a separate agreement with the customer and manages their own service delivery. At the other end of the spectrum, one partner holds most of the power in the partnership. Collaboration on Sales Opportunity is usually at the discretion of the more powerful partner. This partner typically controls the final sale process and will contract directly with the specific customer while the other partner receives payment from the proceeds of the sale.

This second type of partnership is more common. An example comes from a MarTech company that provides a Mobile Marketing Automation (MMA) solution that augments the Salesforce Marketing Cloud, actually replacing Salesforce's own MMA functionality. Salesforce sources and nurtures Sales Opportunities only looping in its smaller technology partner to assist with the sale. The contract is written between Salesforce and the customer. The MMA company still has control over pricing although this is not always the case in such partnership situations. Regardless of the power imbalance in this example, both partners gain significant benefit. Salesforce improves the probability of conversion to a paid subscriber and of retention by selling a feature that is superior to their in-house product. The MMA company gains credibility from partnering with one of the most powerful technology brands in the world in addition to the opportunity for incremental revenue.

RESELLING PARTNERSHIP

Reselling Partnerships involve a partner that distributes the product on behalf of the SaaS company. In effect, the distribution partner purchases the SaaS company's product and sells it at a marked-up price to the customer. The customer contract is with the distribution partner; the SaaS company has no legal relationship with the customer. Resale partners are typically software vendors, system integrators (SIs), and professional service firms. Computer Discount Warehouse, more commonly known as CDW, is a traditional reseller that started with hardware and adding software and SaaS as these products matured. Cybersecurity company Druva has an active Reseller Partner network with regional services firms such as AnylinQ (the Netherlands), LAN2LAN (United Kingdom), and Modo Networks (Dallas). SIs, such as CapGemini, IBM, and Accenture, purchase and resell SaaS products and provide integration services.

Variations on the Reselling Partnership are known as Original Equipment Manufacturer (OEM) and Value-Added Reseller (VAR). In OEM or VAR arrangements, the reseller bundles the SaaS product with other hardware and software items for the purchaser, thereby adding value to the original product. The difference between the OEM and the VAR is that the former combines hardware and software; the latter bundles purely SaaS products. Some VARs offer implementation services as well.

A good OEM Partnership example is that employed by enterprise cloud platform services provider Nutanix. The company's main offering, the Nutanix Cloud Platform (NCP), powers its customers' private clouds. Nutanix is pivoting to a SaaS business model. It currently makes the NCP available for an on-premise bundled hardware and software offering and for a public cloud environment such as Amazon Web Services through Nutanix Clusters. Nutanix actually uses two types of OEM resellers— branded and white label. It has two branded reseller partnerships: Super Micro Computer, Inc. and Flextronics, who pre-install the NCP software on Nutanix-branded hardware. White-label resellers include Dell, Lenovo, IBM, Fujitsu, HP, and Inspur. These companies add the Nutanix product to their hardware and software solutions without disclosing the Nutanix brand name. While this example highlights the company's OEM channel, the bulk of Nutanix's revenue comes from standard Reseller Partnerships. In fact, two resellers, Arrow Electronics and Tech Data Corporation, made up 29% and 14%, respectively, of Nutanix's fiscal year 2020 total revenue.

A good VAR example comes from campaign marketing provider SendGrid. This company embraced the Reseller Partnership strategy by reselling their email Application Product Interface (API) and, later, their marketing campaign services to public cloud providers such as AWS, Azure, and Heroku; SaaS companies such as Twilio and GitHub; and professional services firms such as Deloitte Digital as a SaaS offering for their customers. With a perfectly executed Reseller Strategy, SendGrid was able to achieve an extremely sales-efficient model and outperform their peers. Sales and Marketing expenses as a percentage of revenue was only 25% in fiscal year 2017 at revenues of $112 million. This rate represents a significant difference compared to that of its peers who spend 60% at that revenue level. The SendGrid example also highlights another strategic benefit. With its technology embedded in Twilio's platform, SendGrid was able to demonstrate its value added to the reseller. Twilio quickly realized the revenue and expense synergies to be had and acquired SendGrid on February 1, 2019.

These types of Partnerships can add tremendous value in the form of incremental revenue gained with improved sales efficiency if properly executed. However, before launching a Partnership strategy, companies must evaluate the pros and cons.

PARTNERSHIP PROS AND CONS

A Partnership strategy must balance the benefits and the risks to gain maximum benefit for the effort. The most direct benefit is incremental revenue generated through this channel for the cost of a commission fee as well as the investment in time and resources internally. A partnership can also convey a degree of credibility and trust if the partner is a known brand and this affiliation supports the GTM strategy. At the top of the sales funnel, the partnership should drive increased brand awareness and knowledge of the product's value added. Funnel conversion rates should be higher because the leads arrive with intent and, therefore, require less hands-on nurturing by ISRs. The sales cycle through to paid subscription should be shorter as well. The Marketplace strategy should benefit as well for all of these same reasons. Finally, because the partner owns the front end of the service delivery process, the customer success workload will be lower.

This strategy certainly comes with risks, mainly that companies relinquish control over much of the sales cycle and service delivery. At the earliest stage of the sales cycle, there will likely be little information about the sales pipeline's efficacy and predictability. The partner's pipeline may have a lot of Sales Opportunities, but it's anyone's guess how these leads fit with the company's Ideal Customer Profile or their interest in engaging. This makes it difficult to assign sales resources and to forecast revenues. Partners always make the first contact, and so companies lack direct control over the messaging and branding. If partners don't use your sales-enablement materials and don't stick to the standard talking points, potential customers may dismiss your product out of hand. There will likely be no opportunity for the sales team or management to intercede and save the sale. Even worse, such potential customers may get a negative impression of your product, potentially eliminating this opportunity for your company.

There are also risks when a Sales Opportunity converts to a paid subscriber. The fact that the partner sits between your company and the customer makes direct interactions difficult. Mechanically, it may be difficult to access customer behavioral data if systems are not fully integrated. Thus, the engineering and product teams won't incorporate this data into the product roadmap, potentially limiting innovation. The partner runs the customer success activity, so your company may not have a chance to provide the contracted, or even expected, level of support, leading to higher and more unpredictable churn.

Another risk is *channel conflict*. This term refers to any number of problems that arise when two sales teams are selling to the same target customer. The partner may lead with an emphasis on their product, not yours. If they lose a deal, it may be because the potential customer did not want the partner's product even if they were inclined to purchase yours. Another common issue arises when one potential customer receives inbound calls from both partners. These situations cause external and internal problems. Externally, the potential customer may get turned off by multiple sales calls and may be confused regarding the value added if the messaging differs. Internally, such negative feedback will sow discord among the responsible teams at both the partner and the company. And both teams will argue over the sales commission, putting you in a position where you may need to commission your own team as well for the same deal.

There is also the risk that the two companies in a partnership become so closely coordinated that your company may not be able to work on other sales opportunities not defined by the partnership agreement or to collaborate with other companies in the same space.

At a high level, a Partnership strategy can drive sales efficiency but comes at the cost of less control over the sales and service delivery processes.

Professional Services

Enterprise SaaS companies employ large professional services organizations due to the complexity of the software. Although SaaS customers only need to provide their employees with browsers, they still need services for implementation, specifically integration with other internal systems and user training. Professional services organizations have specific metrics for measuring the level of service provided with the software as well as the speed of onboarding new customers. A good onboarding is critical because it's the first time the end users, e.g., customer's employees, will begin using the software. So our objective is to sell the right level of services to ensure fast implementation.

The following metrics provide an early indication of the customer's happiness.

Professional Services Attach Rate (PSAR)—The PSAR measures the Professional Services Bookings Value divided by

Total Subscription Software Bookings. The PSAR depends on the profitability of the services as well as the total number of hours required for implementation. In my experience, the PSAR should be between 20% and 40%. Further, profitability should be around 40%. A high PSAR could mean that we are pricing correctly or it could mean that our software is not yet mature enough for easy implementation. A low PSAR could mean that we are heavily discounting services to sell the software, or it could mean that the software product has the features and functionality to support rapid implementation. Carefully evaluate PSAR to ensure that you are operating efficiently.

Time to Go Live (TGL)—The time it takes to complete implementation so that customers can begin using the software (Go Live). The TGL date is often used as the revenue recognition date for Enterprise SaaS companies because the company fulfills the delivery requirement in addition to other revenue recognition elements—evidence of a contract, fixed or determinable price, and reasonable assurance of payment.

Time to Live (TTL)—An alternative acronym for TTGL.

Time to Value (TTV)—The time it takes to get customers to realize the full extent of value from the product. The TTV definition depends on the specific service you sell. Here's one example: Consider an Enterprise SaaS business that sells a subscription license based on seats and that the average customer buys fifty seats. Upon implementation, only a fraction of the seat licenses may be in use, say ten. We refer to these seats as active and the remainder as inactive. The Customer Success team will attempt to grow the active seat count to the full subscription license of fifty seats. In this case, TTV could be the date at which all fifty seats are in use.

Time to Grow (TTG)—The time it takes to expand the ACV of the customer via upselling and/or cross-selling. Both the professional services and customer service teams drive this metric. Ease of implementation, which is the professional services objective, and high customer satisfaction, which is the function of the customer success team, make it easier for the sales team to sell more seats to the same organization within the customer (up-selling) and for selling the software to other internal organizations.

New Feature Adoption—This metric straddles Professional Services and Customer Success because one of the other (or both) of these departments can affect this metric. The New Feature Adoption can be measured as the median time it takes for all, or some target level, of the products' users to adopt the feature and the percentage of users who utilize the new feature. As the feature matures, then you should use traditional Customer Success metrics to measure engagement.

Key Takeaways

- An Enterprise SaaS company employs a Direct Sales team to sell its software and professional services. This GTM strategy represents a significant investment because it requires a large team consisting of AEs, partnership managers, product knowledge experts, and administrative employees using Customer Relationship Management software, with the entire team led by an experienced leader, the Chief Revenue Officer.

- This heavy investment requires close review and reporting by the finance team to ensure the company earns a superior return on investment. The finance and sales teams must develop a collaborative relationship to ensure best practice metrics reporting are followed.

- Partnerships can leverage this GTM investment, but partners must be chosen carefully and managed properly. The finance team must implement the proper metrics to help the company evaluate partnership success.

- Enterprise SaaS companies require Professional Services teams that must be managed and reported as a separate business because Gross Margins from this activity can easily drag down the consolidated Gross Margin of the company. Professional Services are sometimes offered at deep discounts as an incentive to acquire customers. This is an acceptable practice, but it must be a strategic business decision.

CHAPTER 9

ENTERPRISE SAAS METRICS

Enterprise SaaS companies also require a specific set of SaaS metrics. Higher ACV contracts, annual terms, up-front payments, and time to onboard new customers require a special focus on Top-Line metrics. Measuring the GTM strategy performance requires metrics for sales, marketing, professional services, and customer success. The high expenses associated with the Direct Sales strategy needs special focus. The performance of customer retention is measured for customer dollar churn and expansion. The sum of all these activities will be seen in the CLTV/CAC ratio, although it requires some specific adjustments for Enterprise SaaS companies.

Top-Line Metrics: Bookings, Billings, CARR, and ARR

Bookings, Billings, ARR, and CARR (see Chapter 3) are important metrics for Enterprise SaaS companies because the timing differs between all four metrics.

Bookings is defined as the dollar value of the contract and is recorded at the annual amount, i.e., ACV on the contract signature date. Billings is defined as the percentage of the ACV invoiced and is recorded at the time the invoice is issued. For Enterprise SaaS companies, the Booking Date typically occurs before the Billing Date.

ARR is a standard metric for all SaaS companies. For Enterprise SaaS companies, the time to implement the product delays revenue recognition and, therefore, ARR. So we use a derivative called CARR, which is simply the sum of all Bookings for the history of the company, adjusted for churn and contraction. If we have a high degree of confidence in successful implementation, then we use CARR and use the contract signature date to begin recording CARR. Use caution when reporting this because both the duration of the implementation and the growth rate will create differences between CARR and ARR. I have seen this range from 5%–40%. Larger variances will require that you define the drivers in your reporting.

Just as these four measures—Bookings, Billings, ARR, and CARR—represent a source of funds to the company, the associated liability, i.e., the responsibility to implement and support the product as defined by the contract, is accounted for as Deferred Revenue. This is an account used to record the ACV for which the company is liable for servicing. By reporting on all five metrics, you link your non-GAAP and GAAP measures.

The Economics of a Direct Sales Strategy

The capacity of the Direct Sales approach can be illustrated with a unit economic analysis for a single new customer. We'll start with a review of the unit economics on a range of ACVs from $100,000 to $250,000 to show how Direct Sales works for the Enterprise SaaS company and then show how it becomes more difficult at lower ACV deals. The key component of the Direct Sales GTM strategy is the AE. The AE is the key customer-facing member of the Direct Sales team, responsible for working one-on-one with potential customers in closing deals to create new customers. An AE earns a base salary and a commission on the sales of the company's product. The sales commission compensation is designed to generate 50% of the AE's total earnings if the AE meets a specific sales target, called a Sales Quota. The Sales Quota is almost always an annual target. If the AE exactly meets the Sales Quota, then the total earnings are referred to as OTE. At OTE, 50% of the total compensation comes from salary and 50% from sales commission. The OTE is a key metric because the annual quota is set at a multiple of four to six times OTE. This ratio is important because it drives the main cost component in sales and marketing as we'll see below.

For this theoretical exercise, we assume:

- The contract has a $125,000 ACV.

- Each contract has a Subscription Gross Margin of 78%.

- BCR of 10% with an additional 6% for overhead, i.e., sales leadership, sales support, and administrative activities.

- Sales representative OTE split 50%-50% sales commission and base salary, with the sum grossed up by 25% for taxes and benefits, i.e., fully loaded.

- Onboarding costs are equal to the cost of Professional Services, which is assumed to generate revenue at 40% of Subscription Revenue and operates at 40% gross profit margin.

- Cost per Lead (CPL) of $208 and a 6% Lead to Close conversion rate.

- Each sales representative carries a $1,500,000 annual ACV quota and has OTE of $300,000. At a $125,000 ACV, the AE needs to close one deal per month to make their annual quota. This new customer acquisition pace is typical for Enterprise SaaS companies.

A new customer at a $125,000 ACV generates $97,500 in annual profit and costs $30,000 to onboard. The AE's fixed compensation for this specific deal can be estimated by dividing the ACV of this deal into the AE's quota. So by closing on a $125,000 ACV contract the AE retires 8.3% of annual quota. So we allocate 8.3% of the AEs annual base salary to this deal. Our BCR assumption results in a $12,500 commission on this deal.

Allocating the AE commission and base salary to this contract puts salary and commission at $8,000 each for a total unloaded cost of $25,000 and $31,250 fully loaded cost with taxes and benefits expenses. The Direct Sales team leadership and supporting staff earn commissions on this sale. In my experience, this overhead commission rate equals about 6% of the ACV in aggregate. The overhead costs $20,625 for this sale.

The result is that the Direct Sales model costs the company $85,342 or 68% of ACV in Sales and Marketing expenses and produces $12,158 in contribution profit or 9.7% in contribution margin to fund the company's other operating expenses. By repeating this exercise for the full ACV range from $100,000 to $250,000, you will find that contribution margin is consistent with this result.

We can check our analysis by calculating the CLTV/CAC metric. A $125,000 ACV deal with a 78% gross margin, assuming an eighteen-month average customer lifetime, divided into $85,342, gives a 1.7x CLTV/CAC ratio. Thus, this specific deal generates $1.70 for each $1.00 in Sales and Marketing investment.

So, again, the Direct Sales model can deliver respectable sales performance for this level of ACV.

Theoretical Contribution Margin for a Direct Sales GTM Strategy at a $125,000 Annual Contact Value

Annual Contract Value	$ 125,000
Subscription Gross Margin	78%
Subscription Gross Profit	$ 97,500
Contribution Expenses	
Sales Commission	$ 12,500
Base Salary	$ 12,500
Total Direct	$ 25,000
Fully Loaded	$ 31,250
Overhead	$ 20,625
Total Sales Expense	$ 51,875
Total Marketing Expense	$ 3,467
Total Sales & Marketing Expense	$ 55,342
Total S&M Margin	44%
Onboarding Costs	$ 30,000
Total Contribution Expense	$ 85,342
Total Contribution Expense %	68%
Total Contribution Margin	$ 12,158
Total Contribution Margin %	9.7%
CPL	$ 208.00
Conversion Rate	6.00%
Marketing Cost per New Customer	$ 3,467

The second part of this analysis is to look at the Contribution Margin for deals with an ACV below $100,000. Our annual sales quota assumption begins to break down with deals priced between $50,000 and $100,000. Specifically, a product priced at $50,000 would require the AE to close 2.5 deals per month to meet a $1,500,000 annual quota, and this is an unreasonable number of deals to expect one person to close. The upper limit on annual new customer count for one AE is around fifteen. This number of deals at a $50,000 average ACV means an annual Sales Quota of $750,000. The AE would make $195,000 in this arrangement, but the theoretical Contribution Margin falls to just 3.6%. Any change to the negative would easily make this strategy unprofitable. At these lower price points, Enterprise SaaS companies need to incorporate more sales-efficient strategies.

Customer Retention Metrics

Unit economic measures for customer retention are the same as those for all other types of SaaS companies; we use the common gross and net churn and retention rates. There are two important differences to note.

First, Enterprise SaaS companies typically have robust expansion activity, e.g., increasing spending by their customers throughout the contract term. This increased spending can come from two sources. First, customers may add more users to their current product contract. This is known as Upsell Expansion. Second, customers may purchase additional products from the provider. This is known as Cross-Sell Expansion. When reporting on Expansion rates, we will separate out Upsell and Cross-Sell Expansion. Small/Mid-Market and B2C SaaS companies typically offer a point solution, which may have limited features and functionalities (fewer Cross-Sell opportunities) or may sell only to an individual or small group of users (fewer Upsell opportunities).

Second, Enterprise SaaS companies have higher ACV contracts and lower customer counts than other SaaS companies. Therefore, we base all customer retention rate reporting on dollars and not customer count. The inverse is true for companies serving Small and Mid-Market companies and consumers.

CUSTOMER LIFETIME VALUE TO CUSTOMER ACQUISITION COST

The CLTV/CAC calculation is much more complex for Enterprise SaaS companies because the long sales cycle makes it difficult to attribute Sales and Marketing expenses in one period to new customers in the period of the calculation. The better solution is to report the *Sales Efficiency* metric using the Sales and Marketing expenses in the same period as the New Subscription Bookings, whether actual or forecasted. For example, if you project $20 million in New Subscription Bookings for a given fiscal year, then your Sales and Marketing expenses should, in theory, be ~$20 million to achieve a 1.0x ratio. Since customer count is small relative to Bookings for earlier stage companies and the quarter-to-quarter sales seasonality, the CLTV/CAC calculation will vary widely from one quarter to the next. You will see the same volatility in your CAC Payback Period.

Theoretical Financial Profile SaaS Metrics

Let's return to our theoretical company financial profile and add two customer assumptions that will allow us to calculate SaaS metrics. These are the average ACV and average Customer Lifetime. Then we will take a look at CLTV/CAC, Sales Efficiency, and Magic Number calculations for this business.

For our theoretical business, we will use specific ACV and Customer Lifetime assumptions for each year of the five-year time frame because they will change as the company matures. In year one, product sales have a low price point relative to their potential value added. Even though the company should be able to charge six figures for one customer and gain at least a one-year commitment, several factors limit its ability to achieve this price point and annual contract term. The company does not have a track record of performance at this stage; new customers are taking a risk on its product. Potential customers may not truly understand the value added and need more time to see how others use it. As a new product, it competes with existing products, which, though not as valuable to the customer, have greater awareness and more credibility. These *substitute products* make for a competitive environment. Finally, we will expect to see higher churn among initial customers because of a disconnect between the stated value added and the actual performance. This may be because the product is not robust enough. Or it may be because the pricing did not match value added. Either way, the Customer Lifetime will suffer. As a result of these factors, the company will need to sell at a discount and offer shorter term contracts to acquire its first customers. As the company gains experience and credibility, it can begin to demand higher price points and longer term contracts.

ACV:

- Year 1: $60,000 average ACV

- Year 2: $84,000 average ACV with several new customers paying six figures

- Year 3: $120,000 average ACV

- Year 4: $132,000 average ACV

- Year 5: $150,000 average ACV

As you can see, the company finally achieves an average ACV in the six figures in year three. New customers this year are paying more for the product; existing customers are expanding their use of the product and allocating more of their IT budget to it.

Customer Lifetime—Customer Lifetime is a function of contract term and retention. Contracts keep customers active for a certain period of time while Customer Success ensures customers renew. Similar to the ACV trajectory, we'll start with a relatively average short Customer Lifetime and increase it over the five-year period for all of the same factors. For year one, we'll assume an average Customer Lifetime of 1.2 years, and this grows to just shy of two years.

The CLV for this business is a function of the Gross Margin, average ACV, and Customer Lifetime. Thus, in year one, we calculate CLTV as:

$$\$60,000 \text{ (ACV)} \times 70\% \text{ (Gross Margin)}$$
$$\times 1.2 \text{ years (Customer Lifetime)} = \$50,400 \text{ CLTV}$$

This means that the average year-one customer has a net present value of $50,400.

The CAC is the amount of Sales and Marketing expenses incurred to acquire $1,200,000 in New Subscription Bookings. Because we are modeling an Enterprise SaaS business, we will use Sales and Marketing expenses from the same period. Using the average ACV assumption of $60,000 means that we acquired twenty new customers in year one. Thus:

$$\$677,000 \text{ (sales and marketing cost) } /$$
$$20 \text{ (new customers acquired) } = \$33,869 \text{ CAC}$$

Combining the CLTV and CAC as calculated above gives us a ratio of 1.5x, i.e., $50,400 / $33,869.

CLTV = $60,000 (ACV) x 70% (gross margin) x 1.2 years (customer lifetime) = $50,400

CAC = $677,000 (sales and marketing cost) / 20 (new customers acquired) = $33,869

Customer Lifetime Value CLTV = $50,400 divided by $33,869 = 1.50x

We calculate Sales Efficiency as:

Sales Efficiency = $1.2 million (new subscription bookings) / $677,000 (sales and marketing expense)
= 1.8 (Sales Efficiency)

And finally, the Magic Number:

Annual Change in ARR = $3.2 million - $1 million = $2.2 million

Magic Number = $2.2 million / $677,000 (sales and marketing expense)
= 3.2 (Magic Number)

Saas Metrics	Year 1	Year 2	Year 3	Year4	Year 5
Average ACV	$60K	$84K	$120K	$132K	$150K
Customer Count	20	29	200	1,091	4,800
Magic Number	n/a	3.2	7.4	6.3	5.2
Subscription Gross Margin	70%	72%	75%	77%	78%
Customer Lifetime	1.2	1.4	1.6	1.8	1.9
CLTV / CAC	1.5	1.4	1.7	2.2	2.5
Sales Efficiency Customer	1.8	1.4	1.5	1.6	1.7
Acquistion Cost (CAC)	$34K	$60K	$83K	$84K	$90K
CAC Ratio	$0.56	$0.71	$0.69	$0.63	$0.59
CAC Payback Period in Months	9.7	11.9	11.0	9.9	9.1

The CAC Ratio is the inverse of Sales Efficiency. It reads as the amount of Sales and Marketing investment required to generate $1.00 of New Subscription Bookings. For year one, our hypothetical company spent $0.56 to acquire $1.00 of New Subscription Bookings.

The CAC Payback Period is the time required for an average deal to recover the investment in associated Sales and Marketing and is usually expressed in months. Again, for Enterprise SaaS, we will use figures from the same period. In our example, the average new customer costs $33,869 to acquire. Once the new customer generates revenue, it contributes a gross profit of $42,000 per year (ACV of $60,000 × 70% gross margin for year one) or $3,500 per month. Dividing $3,500 into $33,869 gives 9.7 months, meaning that the average new customer generates enough profit at the gross margin level to recover the average CAC in ten months. The CAC Payback Period does not have a time element in that it does not account for Customer Lifetime. Therefore, it needs to be a reference point for the Customer Lifetime. In this case, for year one, the Customer Lifetime must be higher than ten months for the company to cover the associated CAC.

Enterprise SaaS Example: Crowdstrike

Cybersecurity company Crowdstrike serves as a perfect example of an Enterprise SaaS company. According to the company's most recent SEC filing, for the fiscal year ending January 31, 2022, Crowdstrike counted sixty-one of the Fortune 100 and thirty-seven of the top 100 global companies as customers. Customers include financial giants such as Credit Suisse and Goldman Sachs, entertainment giant Sony, gaming companies SEGA and Pokemon, human resources management software provider Automatic Data Processing (ADP), healthcare provider

Driscoll Health System, Australia's largest telecommunications provider Telstra, automobile e-commerce business Copart, and manufacturer TDK Electronics.

Crowdstrike's GTM strategy consists of a Direct Sales team supported by channel partners. The company also grows revenue with a Land and Expand model and has been very successful in maintaining Dollar-Based Net Retention (DBNR) above 120% for many years. This GTM strategy and performance is consistent with the best-in-class Enterprise SaaS companies.

Crowdstrike's advanced cybersecurity software is extremely complex. Crowdstrike's cloud-native Security Cloud collects reams of data from all of the customers' internal and external lines of communication, identifies cyberthreats, and develops real-time responses to protect against these threats. The company's Falcon Platform facilitates customers' use of the Security Cloud and enables customers to access twenty-two additional security modules. Pricing is based on the number of endpoints and the number of security modules purchased by the customer. Through the Falcon Platform, Crowdstrike can sell more endpoints and additional modules, i.e., both Upsell and Cross-sell.

Like all Enterprise SaaS companies, Crowdstrike employs a Professional Services team to onboard new customers by implementing the software and integrating it with the customer's existing technology stack. Onboarding pricing is on a time and materials basis. Ongoing maintenance and support services are offered as a separate contract.

Average ARR was $106,055 from a subscription customer base of 16,325. The majority of the customer base pays up front annually as you would expect from an Enterprise SaaS company. Crowdstrike's Subscription Revenue dominates at 94% of total revenue with 6% from professional services revenue in the fiscal year ending January 31, 2022. Subscription Revenue Gross

Margin of 78% is exactly in line with the median Gross Margin across public Enterprise SaaS companies. Professional Services gross margin was 44%, which is at the high end of the range among comparable companies.

The SaaS metrics show strong operational execution. One of the most important Enterprise SaaS metrics, DBNR, was 124% for fiscal year 2022 and is consistent with that of comparable companies. This DBNR reflects high Renewal rate and Expansion rate as it is the sum of the two. Crowdstrike's Subscription Revenue mix by type reflects this strong performance. For fiscal year 2022, nearly two-thirds of annual Subscription Revenue was due to renewing customers (42%) and to converting both Upsell and Cross-Sell opportunities with existing customers (24%). Sales Efficiency shows a fiscal year 2022 ratio of 1.29x, which is the highest rate achieved by the company thus far.

Crowdstrike's Operating Margins reflect performance driven by new customer acquisition efficiency, existing customer Retention, and Expansion combined with product dominance and the resulting pricing power. In fiscal year 2022, total Operating Expense (excluding stock-based compensation) made up 64% of total revenue with Research and Development at 19%, Sales and Marketing at 36%, and General and Administrative at 9%. The 65% year-over-year growth in revenue with a high percentage of up-front payments combined with an efficient operating structure boosted FCF to 32%. Thus, the RO40 was 95.

Operating Expense Ratios are consistent with comparable companies with Research and Development at 0.5x of Sales and Marketing and General and Administrative at 0.3x of Sales and Marketing. I think it is useful to point out that these ratios remained nearly unchanged over the past five fiscal years with the average for that period of 0.5 and 0.2.

Crowdstrike, Inc. (CRWD)
Fiscal Year Ended January 31

in $ Thousands	2018	2019	2020	2021	2022
Annual Recurring Revenue	141,314	312,656	600,456	$1,050,051	$1,731,342
Statement Of Operations					
Revenue Subscription	$ 92,568	$ 219,401	$ 436,323	804,670	1,359,537
Professional Services	26,184	30,423	45,090	69,768	92,057
Total Revenue	118,752	249,824	481,413	874,438	1,451,594
Cost of Revenue					
Subscription	39,768	68,519	107,248	173,507	299,860
Professional Services	14,377	17,825	26,667	38,328	51,267
Total Cost of Revenue	54,145	86,344	133,915	211,835	351,127
Gross Margin - Subscription	57%	69%	75%	78%	78%
Gross Margin - Professional Services	45%	41%	41%	45%	44%
Gross Profit	**64,607**	**163,480**	**347,498**	**662,603**	**1,100,467**
Gross Margin	54%	65%	72%	76%	76%
Operating Expenses					
Research & Development	55,458	76,736	114,785	174,396	269,256
Sales & Marketing	102,891	167,507	242,676	350,759	526,912
General & Administrative	25,355	35,596	56,162	80,302	136,895
Total Operating Expenses	**183,704**	**279,839**	**413,623**	**605,457**	**933,063**
Operating Income	**(119,097)**	**(116,359)**	**(66,125)**	**57,146**	**167,404**
Free Cash Flow					
Net Cash Provided by Operating Activities	(58,766)	(22,968)	99,943	356,566	574,784
Net Cash Consumed by Investing Activities	(29,448)	(42,645)	(87,487)	(63,663)	(133,009)
Free Cash Flow	(88,214)	(65,613)	12,456	292,903	441,775
Key Metrics					
ARR	$ 141,314	$ 312,656	$600,456	$1,050,051	$1,731,342
Subscription Customer Count	1,242	2,516	5,431	9,896	16,325
DBNR	119%	147%	124%	125%	124%
ARR/Customer	$ 113,779	$ 124,267	$ 110,561	$ 106,109	$ 106,055
Sales Efficiency	0.80	1.02	1.19	1.28	1.29
Margins					
Gross Margin	54%	65%	72%	76%	76%
Research & Development	47%	31%	24%	20%	19%
Sales & Marketing	87%	67%	50%	40%	36%
General & Administrative	21%	14%	12%	9%	9%
Operating Income (Loss)	-100%	-47%	-14%	7%	12%
Free Cash Flow	-74%	-55%	10%	247%	372%

Source: www.sec.gov regulatory filings

Key Takeaways

- Enterprise SaaS companies use CARR because it better accounts for the run rate SaaS revenue than does ARR. The reason is that the time to onboard new customers and begin revenue recognition takes more than one month. So calculating ARR from the month's recognized recurring revenue understates the true business performance at that point.

- The Unit Economics of a Direct Sales GTM strategy shows that Contribution Margin, which is the net of revenue and all Sales and Marketing activities, is low, approximately 10% in our example. This exercise highlights the need to closely measure and manage this GTM strategy.

- The Sales Efficiency ratio is more relevant to the Enterprise SaaS company than is the CLTV/CAC ratio due to the difficulty of attributing new customer acquisition to sales and marketing activities and due to the low customer count.

- Despite the high expenses associated with the Direct Sales team, proper management can deliver superior returns relative to comparable company benchmarks.

- Crowdstrike generates superior business performance and serves as a best-in-class comparable for Enterprise SaaS companies.

Summary of the Enterprise SaaS Model

The Enterprise SaaS business model has distinctive operational and financial characteristics. The software is used by large companies to manage a complex workflow involving hundreds of users and integrations with potentially dozens of other software applications. The sales cycle is long and complex involving multiple customer conversations led by Direct Sales leaders. Direct Sales teams are expensive and require specific employment contracts and sales efficiency metrics for maximizing success in new customer acquisition. The Customer Success team is likewise expensive but is required to drive Retention and Expansion. This organization also has specific metrics not used in other types of SaaS business models. The software's complexity requires the company to field a Professional Services team consisting of high-level engineers and project managers to ensure efficient onboarding. Given that Net Retention success is highly correlated to the customers' experience with onboarding, this organization's performance requires close attention. Since the software must command a high average ACV, payment terms for each contract have a significant impact on working capital.

Each of these characteristics requires the SaaS professional to fully understand Enterprise SaaS business models. Only by measuring the most appropriate SaaS metrics and interpreting the results can you truly serve as a business partner to the CEO, the board of directors, and the management team.

CHAPTER 10

SMALL- TO MID-MARKET FINANCIAL PROFILE AND GO-TO-MARKET STRATEGY

Overview

SMM SaaS companies serve customers with annual revenues of $1 million–$1 billion and an employee base of 100–1,000. Customers of this size, also referred to as Small and Medium Businesses or SMBs, need the same software solutions as Enterprise companies but have resource constraints that prevent them from using the top vendors. The most common resource constraints are staffing and budget. An additional non-financial constraint is the fact that these customers typically lack experience in software procurement and implementation, and this adds friction to the sales cycle.

Customers will want high-touch sales engagement and service delivery but will likely not have the budget necessary for SMM companies to justify providing this level of support. This reality influences the GTM strategy, which relies on a lower overall sales and marketing budget and a higher mix of marketing to sales spending. The GTM organization will consist of a mix of Inside Sales and Direct Sales teams with the latter operating as individual contributors without pre-sales support. Customer success is usually staffed by a mix of customer support, sales, and engineering folks contributing some portion of their time to the

COR. Most of the marketing budget will be focused on Digital Marketing along with some live events and webinars.

The industry dynamics are unique in that SMM SaaS companies live with the risk of being *stuck in the middle.* This phrase was coined by Harvard Business School professor Michael Porter, who used it to describe a company with a product that can't compete with higher end products and is susceptible to competitive pressures from lower cost providers.

Being stuck in the middle drives SMM SaaS companies to invest in one of two strategies. The first option is to move up the value chain by improving product features, functionality, and quality to compete effectively with higher end options. The other option is to outperform lower cost competitors in gaining market share, usually by lowering the price point to gain market share.

Another interesting result of the competitive landscape is that most SMM SaaS companies are either successful in moving up-market or being acquired or liquidated before reaching the public markets. So we don't have many purely SMM public comparables to use for comparisons. Instead, we rely on private company benchmarking sources such as the KeyBanc SaaS Survey and the OPEXEngine database.

Financial Profile

The ACV price range of $10,000–$50,000 shapes SMM SaaS companies' financial profiles. These lower price points influence the GTM strategy, which requires lower labor costs and a greater reliance on one-to-many marketing. Aggregate Gross Margin tends to be higher than that for Enterprise SaaS companies because professional service revenue is a lower portion of overall revenue, but the absolute dollar amount generated does not adequately fund a pure Direct Sales strategy. Instead, SMM SaaS companies use a portfolio approach, giving them more flexibility in managing CLTV/CAC.

Go-To-Market Strategy

The most common strategies for SMM SaaS companies are:

- Direct Sales

- Inside Sales

- E-Commerce Marketplaces

- Partnerships

Some SMM companies may use all four depending on the business model.

DIRECT SALES

Direct Sales is a valuable GTM strategy *if* the company can deploy an enterprise-grade product and sell it at a premium—at least a $50,0000 ACV. Refer to Chapters 6 and 7 for a more in-depth discussion of Direct Sales strategies.

INSIDE SALES

In SMM SaaS companies, the average ACV generated by ISRs is $28,000. Each day, the ISR has a set of targets to accomplish. These include sending thirty emails per day and making twenty phone calls to potential customers on contact lists. These activities should lead to ten meaningful conversations per day with about one in twenty conversations becoming Sales Qualified Leads, of which 15% convert to paying customers. Under these assumptions, an ISR closes 6.7 deals per quarter. At the company's average ACV of $28,000, each ISR can generate $760,000 in total ACV per year.

Theoretical Contribution Model of an InsideSales GTM with an Average Annual Contract Value of $28,000

Unit Economics for One Inside Sales Representative

Annual Base Salary	$	63,000
Variable Compensation	$	63,000
On-Target Earnings (OTE)	$	126,000
Annual Target Quota in ACV	$	760,000
Productivity		66%
Effective Annual Target Quota in ACV	$	500,000
Average Booking Deal in ACV	$	28,000
One Average Deal as % of Target		5.6%
ISR Cost for One Average Deal	$	7,033

The first step in the Inside GTM unit economic analysis is to calculate the average cost required for an average ISR to close an average ACV deal.

Each month, the ISR is measured on opportunities created and opportunities converted to paying customers. Variable compensation is often based on meeting daily and monthly activity targets and sometimes in lieu of commission on new deals.

Analyzing the profitability of a single deal using the data above will help illustrate the parameters required for this GTM strategy to generate sales efficiency. Using the average metrics for an ISR, we can estimate a $500,000 expected quota for planning purposes. The ACV and expected annual quota assumptions imply that the average ISR needs to close seventy-one deals per year, or just under six per month. By closing one deal at a $28,000 ACV, the ISR will achieve 5.6% of expected annual quota. For the company, the cost of a new customer after the ISRs variable and base compensation is $7,033.

From here, we will calculate the Contribution Margin as defined by all of the variable costs associated with acquiring a new customer. The Contribution Margin concept is a unit economics approach in which the unit is defined as a specific operating activity. For this specific analysis, we define the Contribution Margin as the average theoretical Inside Sales profitability for acquiring a new customer.

In our example above, the $28,000 ACV contract generates 78% in gross margin, which is $21,840 in absolute dollars. We need to increase the average ISR salary and commission by 25% to account for taxes and benefits. This gets us to a Fully Loaded labor cost of $8,792. The sales commission plan for the Inside Sales team allocates 3% of the ACV to the sales management; this adds $840 to the sale cost. The sum of all sales activity costs is $9,632.

Theoretical Contribution Model of an InsideSales GTM with an Average Annual Contract Value of $28,000

Unit Economics for One Inside Sales Representative		
Average Booking Deal in ACV	$	28,000
Subscription Gross Margin		78%
Subscription Gross Profit	$	21,840
Contribution Expenses		
ISR Compensation per Deal	$	7,033
ISR Compensation per Deal - Fully Loaded*	$	8,792
Sales Overhead	$	840
Total Sales Expense	$	9,632
Total Marketing Expense	$	5,000
Total Sales & Marketing Expense	$	14,632
Total Sales & Marketing Expense as % of ACV		52%

The Sales & Marketing expense associated with the average ACV deal accounts for 52% of the $28,000 ACV, leaving $7,208 in remaining profit.

We also need to account for the marketing expenses associated with the new customer acquisition. For this analysis, we will add in an estimated Cost per Lead (CPL) as well as the rate at which the lead converts to a paying customer. The CPL depends on the mix of channels used to acquire new customers. Conversion rates vary widely depending on product pricing versus market demand, marketing campaign effectiveness, and the ISRs skill in nurturing the lead to close.

Assuming a $300 CPL and a 6% conversion rate, the marketing cost associated with the sale is $5,000. The sum of the sales and marketing cost is $14,632, which is 52% of the ACV. Combined with hosting and connectivity costs associated with the Subscription revenue, the sales and marketing activity produces a 47% profit margin.

Tracking performance at this level will give you insight into the Inside Sales effectiveness as a GTM strategy.

The COR component used above relates only to the Subscription Revenue (i.e., the hosting and connectivity as well as some customer support, which is minimal for SMM SaaS companies). But we did not account for the professional services work to onboard the customer. These onboarding expenses are typically much lower than that for Enterprise SaaS and may even be zero if the product allows for self-provisioning. In this case, we will estimate onboarding costs in a simplistic approach.

Typical Professional Services revenue makes up 20% of Total Revenue and 25% of Subscription Revenue. A good Professional Services team can generate 40% gross margin, with the remaining 60% attributed to onboarding cost.

In other words, 60% of 25% of the ACV gives a $4,200 onboarding cost. This means that the Contribution Margin is just 11%.

Theoretical Contribution Model of an InsideSales GTM with an average Annual Contract Value of $28,000

Unit Economics for one Inside Sales Representative		
Average Booking Deal in ACV	$	28,000
Subscription Gross Margin		78%
Subscription Gross Profit	$	21,840
Contribution Expenses		
Total Sales & Marketing Expense	$	14,632
Total Onboarding Expense	$	4,200
Total Contribution Expense	$	18,832
Total Contribution Expense as % of ACV		67%
Total Contribution Margin	$	3,008
Total Contribution Margin as % of ACV		11%

Adding in customer onboarding costs shows that the theoretical margin for an average customer acquired by a typical inside sales representative has a mere 11% contribution margin. Even a small negative change in the assumptions can make the contribution margin negative.

This result highlights the dangers of using Contribution Margin. The first problem is that the assumptions are not static. For example:

- A 38% discount in the ACV results in a 0% Contribution Margin.

- Lower ISR productivity of 50% versus 66% makes the sale break even.

- An additional 40 hours of implementation time above budget similarly consumes 11 points of margin.[1]

- A 60% increase in CPL or a 2.25 point drop in conversion rate sends the contribution margin below zero.

The other problem with the Contribution Margin approach is that you may not be seeing the whole picture. It's easy to exclude relevant costs because they are missed, not well understood, or worse, an organizational bias prevents decision makers from fully embracing the true story.

E-COMMERCE MARKETPLACES

An E-commerce Marketplace is an automated, self-provisioning ordering process for low-ACV customers. The objective is to completely remove labor from the sales cycle, relying instead on marketing investment, product functionality, and transactional efficiency to acquire new customers. This use of an E-commerce

---

1   The forty hours referenced is from a simplistic calculation assuming a cost per hour of $75 for a Professional Services person earning $157,500 per year at full utilization.

Marketplace is also referred to as a *marketing-driven* strategy because all leads are generated by marketing investment. There are three key areas in which companies need to be successful in employing this strategy.

MARKETING INVESTMENT
Unlike Direct and Inside Sales, the Marketplace strategy requires marketing to drive brand awareness and education. Brand awareness campaigns are designed to connect with target customers and build trust. Common strategies are blogging, email marketing, host-read podcast advertising, influencer marketing, and social sharing campaigns. Educational campaigns focus on the value added from your product as well as how to use it. After acquiring customers, companies need to drive user engagement. FAQs and user communities are important, but true engagement requires continual marketing campaigns to remind customers of the value added, to showcase use cases, and to provide tips on working with the product. The objective of post-transaction activity is to completely replace labor-intensive customer support.

PRODUCT FUNCTIONALITY
This often-overlooked objective refers to the necessary product changes required to make the functionality more stand-alone and thus avoid integration and to make the interface more intuitive. Potential customers who buy into the value proposition need to see the ease of use. Further, the product must include product tours and in-application (In-App) tutorials. Product tours provide a "welcome" of sorts and coach the user through tasks that demonstrate the product's specific capabilities. A more in-depth version of the product tour is an interactive walk-through in

which the user is prompted to begin working in the product. In-App tutorials refer to functionality that tracks the customer's behavior and provide related educational advice. The best practice here is to make suggestions or provide tips at various points of frustration in the user's workflow. A basic product combined with automated support features will improve conversion to paid subscriptions and boost retention.

TRANSACTIONAL EFFICIENCY

SaaS companies experience shopping cart abandonment, the main reasons for which are a lack of perceived value and trust in the brand, transaction and application security concerns, lack of payment options, long checkout flow, and transaction errors. Marketing addresses value and trust and, to an extent, security concerns, but SaaS companies need to invest in development resources and third-party software for the other obstacles.

The E-commerce Marketplace is a mass-market, low-cost competitive strategy best employed for point solutions with a low ACV. These market and product characteristics make this strategy best suited for a B2C SaaS company. SMM SaaS companies that successfully employ a Marketplace strategy typically started their businesses serving a mass market with a Point Solution and built a higher value add product as they grew.

Avalara serves as a good example of just such a business strategy. Avalara launched its business in 2004 with AvaTax, a simple solution for sales taxes, and added functionality as it matured. Within ten years, the company penetrated the middle market, earning 80% of its revenues from these customers with an average ACV of $16,115. By 2019, Avalara grew the average ACV for this market segment to $23,758, reflecting the higher value added from its products. The company still maintains an active

Marketplace, which obviously serves to generate revenue but also as a way to build its user community. Growth in the user community increases the pool of accountants and bookers skilled in Avalara. These users create demand for the product when they move to companies that do not use Avalara, multiplying sales efforts.

PARTNERSHIPS

As we saw in the Enterprise SaaS section, a GTM strategy that leverages partnerships with other companies can make a huge impact in lowering CACs and achieving scale. Because of their financial constraints, SMM SaaS companies typically use Co-Marketing and Affiliate partnerships.

CO-MARKETING PARTNERSHIPS

A Co-Marketing program requires the least effort and, consequently, entails the least revenue upside. In this arrangement, a company works with another player in the same space and with similar target customers by collaborating on marketing events and content creation. Nearly all companies have some type of co-marketing program. It may simply be the placement of select customers' logos on the website or co-sponsoring a webinar in which employees of both companies present content. Co-Marketing programs typically do not involve a monetary element. Increment revenue is derived indirectly through higher social media profile and brand awareness. Success is hard to measure, but the incremental cost is typically small.

AFFILIATE PARTNERSHIPS

An Affiliate program involves a fee for referral arrangement with third parties that are in contact with target customers. The Affiliate earns a commission for sourcing leads on behalf of the SaaS company.

The Intuit QuickBooks Affiliate Program serves as a prime example. The program pays registered partners a fee for new customers and new leads. Partners place the QuickBooks logo and link on a web page and are paid when customers use this link to engage with QuickBooks either as paid subscribers or free-trial users. For its QuickBooks software product, Intuit pays its partners:

- A commission of 7% of ACV for monthly net sales of up to $10,000 and 10% for net sales above this level.

- $25 for each new free-trial sign-up for QuickBooks Online.

- $25 for each new Intuit Online Payroll subscriber.

- A 10% commission for all QuickBooks supplies purchased using the affiliate's web page link.

This well-defined Affiliate program highlights Inuit's strategic priorities. The company is seeking to monetize its legacy perpetual software product and this is why it pays a commission on the incremental revenue. It assigns a higher priority to growing the SaaS business and willingly pays for leads, only some portion of which will convert. So there's marketing investment in the online product but not the perpetual product. The strategy is paying off with perpetual product, the *Desktop*

Ecosystem, revenues declining slightly while for the SaaS product, the *Online Ecosystem*, revenues grew 21% year-over-over from fiscal year 2019 to fiscal year 2020. The lesson in this example is that the Affiliate program should be carefully established to align with the company's priorities.

Key Takeaways

SMM SaaS companies are typically private companies with annual revenues of less than $100,000. The products typically generate an average ACV of between $10,000 and $50,000. Lower product pricing, even with high margins, provides fewer absolute dollars to fund marketing investment than those in Enterprise SaaS companies. By crafting a portfolio of sales channels and managing the ROI by channel, companies can achieve a high degree of scale for their Sales and Marketing investments.

Common sales strategies include:

- Direct sales only if the software offering commands an ACV greater than $50,000.

- Inside sales, which is the dominant strategy for SMM SaaS companies, is a lower cost sales strategy that relies on marketing lead generation.

- E-commerce marketplace is a marketing-driven strategy that relies on automated sales and customer self-provisioning.

- Partnerships:

- Co-marketing: A collaboration between two companies for marketing events or content creation

- Affiliate: A relationship in which one company pays another for referrals

These GTM strategies are designed to generate profit at the Contribution Margin level. As we saw with Enterprise SaaS companies, this margin is thin and must be closely measured and managed.

The finance team must be heavily involved in capturing and reporting these metrics to management, which, in turn, can use these insights to drive the addition of technology features that reduce sales friction and lower customer support expenses. Thus, measuring and managing these metrics can drive improved business performance.

CHAPTER 11

SMALL- TO MID-MARKET SᴀᴀS METRICS

As we learned above, Enterprise SaaS companies rely almost exclusively on direct sales. These companies use other channels, but the Direct Sales team drives the unit economics. SaaS professionals who master Direct Sales planning and reporting will understand the main profitability lever. Not so in SMM SaaS companies, which compile and use a portfolio of marketing channels. Typically, an individual channel does not dominate sales activities, so SMM SaaS companies need to monitor and manage all channels.

SMM SaaS companies also need to track the percentage of users who are paying as well as the rate of user conversion from free trials to paid subscriptions. ROI should be calculated for each marketing campaign.

SMM SaaS companies typically use digital marketing for lead generation, and this requires tracking of marketing campaigns with metrics such as email opens and ad click through rates. The inside sales team conducts webinars as a cost-effective way to educate and convert potential users, so webinar performance must be monitored as well.

SMM SaaS Model Example: Hubspot, Inc.

Hubspot is a good example of an SMM SaaS company because their average ACV is $10,000, and their GTM strategy consists of inbound, partnerships, and freemium, with straightforward software that can be self-provisioned. The company has been very successful in growing its ACV by enhancing its software and targeting larger accounts. It was a portfolio company of Matrix Partners whose well-known SaaS influencer, David Skok, led the investment. All SaaS practitioners owe a great debt to Mr. Skok, who helped introduce and define SaaS metrics and continues to provide guidance and advice to SaaS professionals.

Hubspot provides three main offerings—a cloud-based platform for marketing (Marketing Hub), sales (Sales Hub), and customer services (Services Hub)—as well as a website hosting and management tool (CMS Hub) and a business process automation product (Operations Hub). The three main hub offerings have three pricing tiers, which are called Starter, Professional, and Enterprise. The Sales Hub and Services Hub are priced on a per-user basis; the Marketing Hub is priced on the number of the customer's marketing contacts.

Pricing is sophisticated enough to match company revenue to customer value add, yet simple for potential customers to understand. You can also see Hubspot seeks to increase the average ACV of its customer base with the Enterprise offering as well as additional product offerings. And Hubspot has been successful with this strategy, increasing average ACV above $10,000.

To improve FCF, Hubspot offers a 10% discount for up-front payments. The company does not disclose the mix of monthly to up-front payments, but its FCF is positive and increased to double digits as a percentage of revenue for the most recent fiscal year.

HubSpot, Inc.
Summary of Product Pricing by Tier

Marketing Hub		
Tier	ACV $s	Pricing Metric
Starter	540	per 1,000 marketing contacts
Professional	9,600	per 2,000 marketing contacts
Enterprise	43,200	per 10,000 marketing contacts

Sales Hub		
Tier	ACV $s	Pricing Metric
Starter	540	2 users
Professional	5,400	5 users
Enterprise	14,400	10 users

Service Hub		
Tier	ACV $s	Pricing Metric
Starter	540	2 users
Professional	5,400	5 users
Enterprise	14,400	10 users

Hubspot generates strong gross margin, which has been in the mid-80th percentile for the past five fiscal years. The company achieved this despite offering professional services at a gross margin loss. Managing services at a loss is quite common in the SaaS business, especially for companies that succeed in reducing professional services as a percentage of revenue (down to 3.4% as Hubspot did in its latest fiscal year).

Fiscal Year Ended December 31
in $ Thousands

	2018	2019	2020	2021	2022
Statement Of Operations					
Revenue					
Subscription	$ 356,727	$ 487,450	$ 646,266	$ 853,025	$ 1,258,319
Professional Services	$ 18,885	$ 25,530	$ 28,594	$ 30,001	$ 42,339
Total Revenue	$ 375,612	$ 512,980	$ 674,860	$ 883,026	$ 1,300,658
Cost of Revenue					
Subscription	$ 50,905	$ 68,242	$ 95,383	$ 126,277	$ 204,835
Professional Services	$ 21,839	$ 27,715	$ 28,619	$ 33,738	$ 44,633
Total Cost of Revenue	$ 72,744	$ 95,957	$124,002	$ 160,015	$ 249,468
Gross Margin - Subscription	86%	86%	85%	85%	84%
Gross Margin - Professional Services	-16%	-9%	0%	-12%	-5%
Gross Profit	$ 302,868	$ 417,023	$ 550,858	$ 723,011	$ 1,051,190
Gross Margin	81%	81%	82%	82%	81%
Operating Expenses					
Research & Development	$ 57,557	$ 94,275	$ 124,489	$ 166,223	$ 240,356
Sales & Marketing	$ 193,843	$ 236,345	$ 304,086	$ 401,5 29	$ 582,268
General & Administrative	$ 44,287	$ 58,400	$ 71,520	$ 84,599	$ 116,604
Total Operating Expenses	$ 295,687	$ 389,020	$ 500,095	$ 652,351	$ 939,228
Operating Income	$ 7,181	$ 28,003	$ 50,763	$ 70,660	$ 111,962
Free Cash Flow					
Net Cash Provided by Operating Activities	$ 49,614	$ 84,851	$ 118,973	$ 88,913	$ 238,728
Net Cash Consumed by Investing Activties	$ {27,347}	$ {33,473}	$ {53,846}	$ {58,873}	$ {61,865}
Free Cash Flow	$ 22,267	$ 5 1,378	$ 65,127	$ 30,040	$ 176,863
Key Metrics					
Subscription Customer Count	41,593	56,628	73,483	103,994	135,442
DBNR	100.5%	100.7%	99.9%	102.3%	115.2%
Revenue/Customer	$ 10,180	$ 9,904	$ 9,920	$ 9,582	$ 10,486
Sales Efficiency	0.53	0.55	0.52	0.51	0.70
Margins					
Gross Margin	81%	81%	82%	82%	81%
Research & Development	15%	18%	18%	19%	18%
Sales & Marketing	52%	46%	45%	45%	45%
General & Administrative	12%	11%	11%	10%	9%
Operating Income (Loss)	2%	5%	8%	8%	9%
Free Cash Flow	6%	10%	10%	3%	14%

Source: www.sec.gov regulatory filings

Operating income, excluding stock-based compensation, turned positive in 2019 and continued to stay in the high single digits as a percentage of revenue. This result is due to Hubspot's exceptional execution of its strategy as an SMM SaaS company. Additionally, Hubspot successfully captured efficiencies of scale. You can see this is the steady reduction in Operating Expense as a percentage of revenue over the past five fiscal years.

Hubspot makes an excellent comparable company for benchmarking purposes and for the study of best practices. I include the full financial profile below.

Key Takeaways

SMM SaaS companies employ a mix of sales channels to drive lead generation and revenue conversion. Successful SaaS professionals are responsible for:

- Monitoring performance of all sales channels

- Tracking the percentage of users who are paying customers

- Tracking rate of user conversion to paid subscriptions

- Calculating ROI for each marketing campaign

- Tracking other metrics for marketing campaigns (i.e., email opens, click-through rates)

- Developing attribution models for webinar performance and providing relevant metrics

We can use Hubspot's performance as an example of best-in-class performance for the SMM SaaS company.

Summary of the Small/Mid-Market Saas Model

The SMM SaaS business model has advantages in that the time and cost to launch products are much lower. And there are a lot of ways to reach customers as we've discussed. Success in the early stages requires a light-touch GTM strategy to ensure sales efficiency and preserve operating dollars for continued product development. In the midterm, these companies must continually monitor the competitive market dynamics to ensure that the product remains compelling and that the Average Selling Price can be maintained and increased. Tactically, the finance team must track the key metrics associated with each GTM channel and continually test and evaluate the effectiveness of each individual channel versus the others. This insight truly enables the company to maximize the effectiveness of its marketing investment.

CHAPTER 12

BUSINESS-TO-CONSUMER FINANCIAL PROFILE

Overview

B2C SaaS companies provide software services tailored to individuals. Some are lifestyle companies such as personal financial lifestyle application Mint and meditation application Calm. There are a whole host of business management tool providers such as Calendly, DocuSign, Dropbox, Hootsuite, Hubspot, Mailchimp, SurveyMonkey, and Zoom. Any company that provides a service to an individual user has a B2C component to their business model even if it sells to businesses.

I'm excluding media companies such as Netflix, Disney+, Hulu, Spotify, Pandora, YouTube, and Twitch, gaming companies such as Playrix and Gameloft, and news outlets such as *The Wall Street Journal* and *The New York Times* because these are B2C *subscription* companies. Certainly, software is part of the service delivery, but the *content* is the primary value add for all of these digital channels. Many of these companies also monetize their content with transaction fees such as pay-per-view content and in-app purchases, and these are non-recurring revenues. As such, these companies do not make good comparables for evaluating the SaaS business.

B2C SaaS companies serve markets characterized by low barriers to entry and low switching costs. Free Offerings such as

Free Trials and Freemium programs make it easy for consumers to engage with the tool. Simply entering a credit card number facilitates customer onboarding. But it's also easy for customers to leave. Billing is monthly, and this means that consumers can easily cancel subscriptions. This often happens when consumers receive their credit card bill, which reminds them that they are paying for a subscription that may no longer be valuable. This is why you will see a spike in cancellations mid-month. Given these industry dynamics, it is important to acquire and to keep paying customers.

B2C SaaS companies employ GTM strategies to drive Brand Awareness as the entry point to access potential consumer leads. More specifically, these companies match heavy Digital Marketing with Free Offerings.

Financial Profile

GROSS MARGIN

B2C SaaS companies generate high gross margins because direct costs are so low. The services are self-provisioned by customers who have very little access to support services. Lists of Frequently Asked Questions (FAQs) require low up-front investment and very little maintenance. Blog posts require routine updates; this is part of your content management strategy, and therefore, its costs sit in Sales and Marketing. Most companies augment FAQs and blogs with very limited support activities, usually providing representatives in low-cost locations via live chat. Hosting and connectivity will be the largest component of COR, but consumer activity typically doesn't require heavy costs for computing, bandwidth, and storage. At scale, with strong execution, B2C companies should generate gross margins above 75%. The low incremental cost to serve is important because it allows for higher Digital Marketing spend and Free Offerings as discussed below.

WORKING CAPITAL TROUGH

B2C SaaS companies' reliance on monthly subscriptions has a significant impact on their working capital needs. This is due to the fact that the company invests in customer acquisition in one period but earns back that investment monthly over several months. And worse, the higher the growth, the greater the working capital needs. This effect is known as the *Working Capital Trough.*

The Working Capital Trough - Working capital requirements increase as growth. Cumulative cash flow by month for six months under three growth scenarios

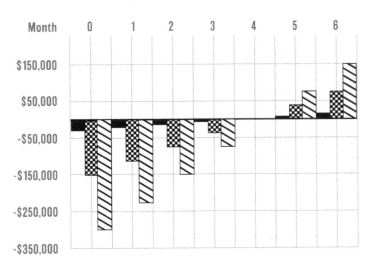

■ No. of new customers = 100
◪ No. of new customers = 500
⊠ No. of new customers = 1,000

Take, for example, a B2C SaaS company that develops and sells subscriptions on a monthly basis. Assume that:

- The company sells an annual software subscription at $1,200.

- This price point ensures an annual gross margin of 75%.

- The CAC is $300.

With these assumptions, the company has a CLTV/CAC ratio of 3.0x with a twelve-month customer lifetime. This means that each month, the company earns $100 in revenue and $75 in gross profit from the average customer, and this profit allows the company to recover all of its customer acquisition investment in four months.

Now let's assume that the company can continue to acquire customers for $300 each at any volume; this implies that the working capital investment increases by $300 for each new customer. Therefore, under this assumption, the company needs $30,000 to acquire 100 customers, $150,000 to acquire 500 customers, and $300,000 to acquire 1,000 customers (as shown in the nearby chart). The Working Capital Trough deepens with increased growth.

Now let's look at the relationship between the Working Capital Trough and the new ARR. Under the three examples above, adding 100 new customers increases ARR by $120,000, adding 500 customers increases ARR by $600,000, and adding 1,000 customers increases ARR by $1,200,000.

By comparing the incremental new ARR to the Working Capital Trough, you will see that the new ARR increases by a factor of four times the investment in acquiring new customers.

Impact on Cash Flow Breakeven by Introducing Annual Upfront Payments

Cumulative Cash Flow by Payment Mix

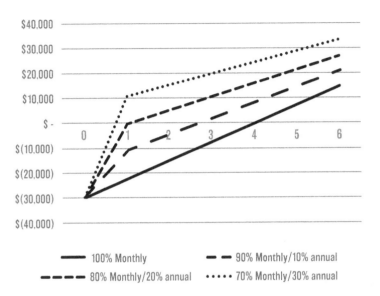

An obvious approach to temper the depth of the Working Capital Trough is to introduce quarterly or annual payments. The impact of quarterly payments is minimal. The depth of the trough and the breakeven month will be the same. Annual payments, on the other hand, make a significant difference. Using the same assumptions above, the impact on working capital is readily visible. Even increasing the mix of annual payments to just 20% of total Billings shortens breakeven by three months. The nearby image shows how an increasing mix of up-front payments can reduce the cash flow break-even point and thus reduce working capital requirements.

The takeaway is that B2C SaaS companies should offer only annual payments in lieu of monthly payments. The impact of the annual billing is so great that it allows plenty of room for incentives. For the example above with 20% annual Billings, holding all other assumptions constant, the company could offer a pricing discount of up to 28.57% and show exactly the same break-even point as in the 100% monthly payments scenario.

In the real world, Hubspot offers a 10% discount for annual prepaid subscriptions. A 10% discount in our scenario does not change the break-even month (although the slope of the line is moderated by 15%).

These exercises assume that there is a 1:1 relationship between CAC and new customer count as the number of new customers acquired in a given month increases. In reality, as the company seeks to add more customers in each period, CAC will grow exponentially. Each incremental customer will cost more than the prior customer. The effect is called the *Law of Diminishing Returns.* This is an economic principle that states that each unit of incremental investment results in a lower ROI. There are two main reasons why this theory applies to customer acquisition:

- *The Total Serviceable Market (TSM) is smaller than your Total Addressable Market (TAM), and readiness to engage varies among targeted consumers.* The TSM is defined as the total set of customers in a given period with a propensity to engage with the product, but these customers have varying propensities to engage. Some may be actively looking to engage already and quickly respond to a marketing campaign. Some of those looking to engage may receive the marketing campaign at the wrong time— they may just be busy. Others may be interested in the product but may not have the awareness or education that would allow them to engage.

- *Competition for the company's users reduces the pool of target consumers.* Competing companies will run marketing campaigns at the same time and may pick up consumers who would normally respond to your marketing and this reduces the TSM. Strength of brand and depth of relationship with potential consumers are material influences, as are the timing of the campaigns and the channels in use. As the pool of target consumers shrinks, the cost to acquire them increases.

As a result, the CAC increases exponentially as companies drive increased customer acquisition. The chart below demonstrates this effect. In our above example, we assumed that each customer can be acquired for $300. As the chart shows, we are able to acquire the first customer at $300 but then need to increase spending to acquire each additional customer, paying $384 for the 500th customer and $510 for the 1,000th customer. The higher CAC will push out the break-even point, exacerbating the working capital needs.

Customer Acquisition Cost (CAC) Growth with Each Incremental Count of New Customers in a Given Period

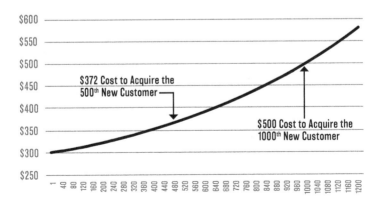

For the finance and marketing teams, mapping the relationship between the investment in new customer acquisition and the resulting new customer count and ARR is a critical tool for understanding the incremental cost of acquiring each subsequent customer. The focus should be on the slope of the line, which will give insights into the TSM and the competitive pressures at work.

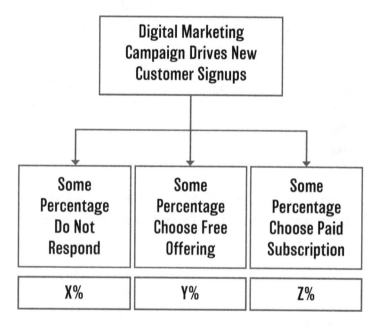

Flow of Potential Customer Response to Digital Marketing Campaigns

For any given marketing campaign, responses will fall into three buckets. Tracking X%, Y%, and Z% will allow you to understand the performance of each campaign. Consolidating the data from all campaigns will give you critical insight into the performance of your digital marketing budget.

Further, the teams need to track the consumer response to each Digital Marketing campaign. Target consumers will respond in one of three distinct ways: some percentage, x, will not respond to this specific campaign; some percentage, y, will choose the Free Offering; and some percentage, z, will go straight to purchasing subscriptions. The combination of x, y, and z will add to 100%. See the nearby flowchart for illustration of this process.

Of those who choose Free Offerings, some percentage (represented by CR%, or Conversion Rate percentage) will convert to paid subscriptions. It's important to note that the CR% differs dramatically between Free Trial and Freemium. Free Trial consumers typically convert at 60% while Freemium consumers will convert at 10%–20%. The CR should be tracked because lower-than-benchmark performance indicates that your TSM is lower than you expected and that you are overspending on an individual marketing campaign. This analysis will also help you evaluate the efficacy of a Free Trial compared to a Freemium Offering.

Understanding these four percentage metrics will allow SaaS professionals to calculate the performance of each individual Digital Marketing campaign and report the ROI for each. Each ROI datapoint should be aggregated for all campaigns to show the ROI of the Digital Marketing budget. A deep understanding of these metrics enables the finance and marketing teams to best manage marketing investment decisions.

Key Takeaways

- B2C SaaS companies provide software services to individual consumers, usually in the form of a mobile application. Challenges in serving this market include low barriers to entry and low switching costs, both of which must be addressed with heavy marketing spend.

- B2C SaaS companies can generate high gross margins because the direct costs of offering the software are so low. The computing power, storage, and connectivity expenses associated with hosting are much smaller per customer as a percentage of MRR than that for other SaaS business models.

- Nearly all of the Sales and Marketing expenses are deployed to generate online customer leads using daily paid digital marketing budgets. This strategy requires daily monitoring because each incremental lead costs more than the prior lead. The steepness of this curve can consume daily budgets without the expected lead generation and cause a negative ROI for the daily marketing campaign.

- The Working Capital Trough is a function of the funds needed to acquire marketing leads before the new customers generate enough profits to offset the CAC. This sales motion is unique to B2C SaaS companies because nearly all payments are invoiced monthly instead of up front on a quarterly or annual basis. Incrementally higher revenue growth requires higher amounts of Working Capital, which ultimately constrain growth because of the time it takes to recover the CAC. The CFO must build a financing strategy using a combination of debt and equity to support the company's growth targets.

- The Working Capital Trough can be addressed with discounts for annual payments. The company must determine the dollar value or the discount that minimizes the Working Capital Trough while preserving operating margins.

CHAPTER 13

B2C GO-TO-MARKET STRATEGY

Marketing Channels are the wide variety of ways in which to reach potential customers. The channel types range from traditional means such as print, radio, and television to live in-person and virtual events to Digital Marketing. Traditional marketing channels are dominated by high-budget marketing departments at large corporations, leaving little room for emerging companies. Digital Marketing is best suited for the latter because it is more cost effective.

Digital Marketing

Digital Marketing is a broad term because it refers to all online channels used to access potential consumers. It forms an essential part of the GTM strategy. We can subcategorize Digital Marketing into several groups.

SEARCH ENGINE OPTIMIZATION (SEO)

SEO refers to the optimization of your company's website for maximum visibility to the search engine algorithm. The objective is to get your website ranked highly for keyword searches that you do not purchase. These non-sponsored website listings are known as organic listings and prospective customers who click on these listings are referred to as Organic Leads. The leads are free; the cost is in the website optimization.

SEARCH ENGINE MARKETING (SEM)

SEM refers to the use of paid advertisements for placement in the results of online searches. Marketers purchase keywords that trigger paid advertisement placement in search results. These leads are called Paid Leads. The single largest provider SEM vendor is, of course, Google through its Google Ads product. Google Ads allows marketers to identify keywords that match the demographic they seek and to place bids on those with the best fit. Facebook allows marketers to run campaigns through its Ads Manager platform. LinkedIn's service is Campaign Manager.

DIGITAL ADVERTISING

Digital Advertising is the practice of purchasing display space on websites to run static or video advertising. Originally referred to as banner advertising due to the selling of the website header space and now called Display Advertising or Sponsored Content, Digital Advertising is typically among the lowest cost Digital Marketing channels because it has limited demographic targeting data.

DIRECT NOTIFICATION

This term refers to email, mobile numbers (SMS/text), and push notifications used to acquire potential subscribers and maintain engagement with current customers. Contact lists are purchased from third-party vendors and collected by the company itself at events such as symposiums, trade shows, panel discussions, and webinars. Email marketing continues to serve as the primary Direct Notification means. However, mobile and push notifications are growing in popularity because this tactic uses customer behavioral data to enhance conversion rates.

CONTENT MARKETING

Content Marketing refers to the creation of proprietary content for social media posts, company-hosted blogs, v-blogs, podcasts and webinars, articles, research papers, and any other material that will capture and maintain the attention of consumers, both before and after the sale. Companies use this tactic throughout the customer journey. Social media content introduces customers to the brand, i.e., Brand Awareness. It serves only to get the company's name and business in front of the decision maker. More in-depth content focuses on the product's value added and therefore provides Customer Education. Technical content such as white papers and case studies are designed for potential customers with a high degree of intent to purchase. Once leads convert to paid subscribers, the onboarding team, typically the professional services or customer success organizations, provide specific content tailored to the customers' use case and skillset. Often, the customer decision maker will need higher level content for the purchase and the end users need help understanding how to best use the product for maximum value added. These activities are typically referred to as Training and Enablement and mark the boundary between marketing and customer success. Finally, as the end users become experts, content still plays a role in furthering their education, thereby increasing engagement and, ultimately, retention.

SOCIAL MEDIA MARKETING

At its most basic, the channel involves establishing a presence on social media and engaging with prospective and current customers alike. Many companies find that their customer engagement is really customer support because disgruntled customers bypass traditional help desk features to reach the company. Although it's important to have a presence, utilizing this channel for lead generation will depend heavily on the specific buyer persona.

AFFILIATE MARKETING

Nearly all companies contract with Distribution Partners or Affiliate Partners that manage a network of websites. SaaS companies will give the partner a specific link to post on their sites. Affiliates are paid for lead generation. Payment method varies from revenue sharing or pay per sale (PPS) to cost per action (CPA), and cost per click (CPM, referring to the pricing in cost per thousand clicks).

INFLUENCER MARKETING

Influencers are individuals who have established a credibility among a specific demographic and who can wield this credibility to drive purchase decisions. In this way, influencers provide products with Social Proof, a term coined by author Robert Cialdini in his 1984 book on persuasion and marketing, *Influence: The Psychology of Persuasion*, to describe this conveyance of credibility. In marketing, a relevant influencer is often someone with a social media presence and a large number of followers. Influencers also come from industry or academia. Influencer Marketing refers to the use of influencers to promote a product. The financial relationship typically takes the form of payment for a product testimonial woven into the influencer's content whether it's an Instagram feed, a YouTube video, or podcast.

Marketers will test each channel to determine which offers the most efficient means of acquiring potential users and invest in the top two to three channels. They will develop channel-specific and consumer-specific *marketing campaigns* and manage them in a way to prevent conflicting messages. Some marketing dollars should be set aside for continual testing of other channels that did not rank highly enough to warrant large investment because the efficacy of these channels may change over time. The marketer's objective is to drive the lowest aggregate Cost per Lead (CPL).

The finance and marketing teams take a role here in evaluating the effectiveness of each channel and each campaign with the ultimate goal of developing an ROI estimate. With this knowledge, the teams can work together to manage the marketing investments. Further, insights from this collaboration may yield data for driving strategy decisions.

Free Offerings

Free Offerings take the form of a **Free-Trial, Freemium,** or just plain **Free** (also known as **Non-Committal** products. Free Offerings allow users to experience the product without risk. Then the company will use various forms of incentives to convert the user to a paid subscription. The company's product team also mines the data on free users' activity for product enhancements as well as to develop features designed to improve conversion rates. Both options provide lead generation in a way that provides for a very efficient GTM strategy, driving down CAC due to lower sales and marketing costs and increasing customer lifetime. Of course, to achieve lower CAC, companies need to focus on marketing effectiveness and product design.

FREE TRIAL

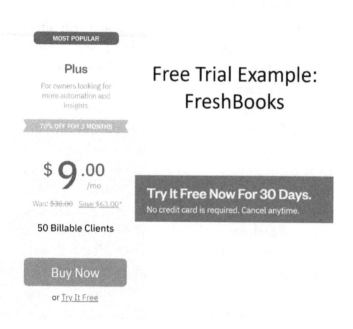

Free Trial Example: FreshBooks

The Free-Trial approach gives consumers use of the basic product for a limited time period, usually fourteen days to one month, and is offered on an Opt-In or Opt-Out basis. The Opt-In Free Trial does not require a credit card to start using the product; instead, consumers enter name, email, and sometimes phone number. Once consumers start the free-trial period, Indirect Sales representatives will attempt to convert these free users to paid subscriptions. The Opt-Out Free Trial requires a credit card to start the subscription; consumers are automatically billed at the end of the period unless they choose to opt out. Free Trials are used by ClearSlide, Canvas, FreshBooks, Flow Microsoft Office 365, and Prezi. In addition to the importance of marketing and product design, a key success factor in the Free-Trial approach is the length of time offered to prospective consumers. There's no right answer here; companies need to evaluate the complexity of the offering and the resulting customers' interaction with the product.

Freemium Example: Trello

The Freemium approach allows consumers to use a light-functionality version of the product for an indefinite period of time during which the users are frequently prompted to upgrade to a paid subscription. Light functionality can mean fewer features or lower storage limits. For example, Trello offers completely free product usage but limits users to ten and the size of attachments to 10MB.

Indirect Sales strategies are typically not used for Freemium product offerings because users have a much lower propensity to convert compared to those in Free Trials. So email marketing is typically used for user engagement. Freemium models are used by lifestyle app Calm, productivity tools Dropbox, Hootsuite, Trello, and Zoom, and most mobile gaming customers.

Free Offerings of a solution reduce the friction with signing up potential paying customers with the goal of driving engagement and conversion to paid subscriptions. Of course, the cost to serve free customers pre-conversion needs to offset the cost to acquire new paying customers to make such a strategy work.

ACCOUNTING FOR FREE TRIAL AND FREEMIUM OFFERINGS

The costs associated with Free Offerings are typically the same as those for paid subscriptions—mainly the direct costs of hosting and infrastructure, which reside in COR. So to ensure accurate financial reporting, the costs of serving non-paying customers should be allocated to Sales and Marketing. Making this allocation will not affect the CLTV/CAC calculation since it uses Gross Margin in the numerator and Sales and Marketing cost in the denominator. However, if the allocation is not made, benchmarking will not be as accurate since both Gross Margin and Sales and Marketing will be lower than that of comparable companies. And the difference can be material. For example, Dropbox does not make this allocation and this resulted in abnormally low gross margins of 33%, 54%, and 67% in fiscal years 2015, 2016, and 2017, respectively. For this accounting methodology, customer support and other third-party data fees are typically not included since these services and features are not offered to free users.

Life Cycle Marketing

B2C SaaS marketing does not end with the conversion to paid subscription. We also need to market to *existing* consumers to drive continued engagement, which lowers churn. Typical techniques for ensuring engagement include email marketing with links to education content, either on the company's blog or video pages. In-app tutorials and product tours help users understand the workflow and features. In-app notifications triggered by specific customer usage can unlock targeted usage suggestions and recommendations. Companies host periodic webinars that often include power users and high-profile industry folks. Paying users can drive new customers if incentivized with a referral bonus. A free month costs next to nothing especially when compared to the average CAC. The strategy of marketing to existing users is referred to as *Life Cycle Marketing*.

Key Takeaways

B2C SaaS companies use a variety of digital marketing channels to reach potential customers including:

- Search Engine Optimization

- Search Engine Marketing

- Digital Advertising

- Direct Notification

- Content Marketing

- Social Media Marketing

- Affiliate Marketing

- Influencer Marketing

Once a potential customer engages, the company offers Free Trials and Freemium Offerings in a bid to convert the lead to a paying customer. Once a customer moves from a free version to a paid subscription, Life Cycle Marketing continues the marketing process to drive continued engagement.

The challenge for the SaaS professional is to create a system and process for monitoring the multiple marketing channels in real time to ensure best use of the marketing budget. Also consider that the optimal mix of channels changes constantly with little notice. Thus, it's a challenge that few B2C SaaS companies can master. However, success in managing this marketing channel strategy can create a long-term competitive advantage.

CHAPTER 14

B2C SAAS METRICS

The CLTV/CAC is the main KPI for B2C SaaS companies. More specifically, companies need to calculate this metric by customer cohort, usually defined as the set of customers acquired in a given month. Because the sales cycle is typically less than one month, the Sales and Marketing expenses can be closely matched to new customers acquired. Once the customer count becomes statistically significant, then the customer lifetime can be precisely defined, completing the necessary components for the CLTV/CAC calculation.

The effectiveness of Free Offerings in generating revenue is monitored for their conversion rates of free to paid users: the average amount of time before converting and the level of user engagement while on the Free Offering.

Be particularly careful in managing Free Offerings because the acquisition cost should include the cost of service delivery such as the computing, bandwidth, and storage costs. Because these costs are buried in the COR, they do not show in Sales and Marketing.

B2C SaaS Company Example: Dropbox, Inc.

Dropbox was founded in 2007 to provide an online file storage hub for consumer data. Although several B2C storage companies launched around this time, Dropbox differentiated itself with a product feature that listed files stored online alongside files stored locally, i.e., on the consumer laptop. For Microsoft users, their Dropbox-hosted files appeared in the File Explorer app exactly as did their laptop files. Whereas competitors required users to login to unique websites with proprietary features, Dropbox allowed users to interact with its product in the same way in which they were already doing. The key learning here is that Dropbox *did not require a change in behavior on the part of the customer*, thereby simplifying adoption. And this product-driven GTM approach allowed the company to emerge as a leader in this space.

As it gained experience in this space, Dropbox realized that customers used the product to collaborate with others, whether or not these individuals had active Dropbox accounts. Dropbox's Free Offering allowed non-users to sign up and view shared documents, thereby embracing the network effect driven by the sharing of files. Users further pushed the network effect as they changed jobs and interacted with separate sets of non-users.

In addition to the product differentiation, the Free Offering was another key to Dropbox's growth. Over the past five fiscal years ending December 2021, 90% of all new paid subscribers converted from the Free Offering. Dropbox aggressively markets to free users with email marketing, in-app notifications, and discounts for converting to paid subscriptions.

Use of a Free Offering is consistent with our B2C SaaS company definition. Dropbox is also a good example because it has other attributes that closely match our definition. Average Annual Contract Value is below $10,000. The product is a point solution, meaning that it solves a specific user problem. Users self-provision the product without any services.

Dropbox uses the term Average Revenue per Unit (ARPU) with a unit defined as a single customer. For the five fiscal years from 2017 to 2021, Dropbox reported ARPU of $111.91, $117.64,

$123.07, $128.50, and $133.73, respectively. The relatively low price point demonstrates the low value add of a file storage and collaboration product. Dropbox's ability to increase user monetization is also limited as evidenced by ARPU growth, which was 3.6% on a Compounded Annual Growth Rate (CAGR) basis for these five periods. To grow total revenue, Dropbox focuses on new customer acquisition. For the same five fiscal years, Dropbox grew paying user count nearly two-and-a-half times faster than ARPU with a CAGR of 8.8%. This growth strategy is very common among B2C companies.

The Gross Margin trend illustrates the impact of the Free Offering. Since the hosting and infrastructure costs associated with serving non-paying users are recorded as direct expenses in COR, the larger the ratio of non-paying to paying users, the greater the negative impact on Gross Margin. According to the company's S-1 filing, the first reported Gross Margin was for fiscal year 2015 and it was only 33%. This metric is far below that of comparable SaaS companies. So the Free Offering dramatically depressed Gross Margin.

For Dropbox to become a public company, it needed to show a Gross Margin equivalent to that of its peer SaaS companies. So to prepare for its IPO, Dropbox made two decisive changes that proved to be the main drivers of this improvement. First, the company invested heavily to build high-performance data centers and consolidated operations into the new facilities. In 2015 and 2016, the company invested over $200 million in capital expenditures for data centers as well as offices and patent purchases. This sum amounts to 14% of revenue for each of those two years. Compare this investment rate to the $24 million capital investment made in 2017; this is only 2% of revenue. Gross Margin also suffered because user data had to be duplicated before being relocated to servers in new facilities. During these two years, the company had to store double the amount of data, and this was another reason for the abnormally low Gross Margin. By 2017, Gross Margin grew to 68% on the strength of the new data center facilities as well as the elimination of duplicate datasets.

Dropbox's second Gross Margin improvement decision was operational in nature. Beginning in 2016, the company started closing accounts of long-inactive users and implemented a policy to close accounts with no activity over the prior twelve months. Inquiries from these users were ignored, freeing up customer support time.

Operating Expense Margins for Dropbox and Comparable Companies Box and HubSpot

Cost Category	Dropbox	Box	HubSpot
R&D	27%	27%	23%
S&M	29%	51%	50%
G&A	17%	15%	14%
Operating Expense Margins with Dropbox Adjustment*			
R&D	27%	27%	23%
S&M	89%	51%	50%
G&A	17%	15%	14%

*Dropbox expense margin proforma analysis incorporating the cost of the free offering, which is the cost of the GTM strategy, in S&M.

Note: Expense margins for these three B2C Saas companies are drawn from their fiscal year with revenue levels near $600M to provide for the most precise comparable company analysis. Margins exclude stock-based compensation. Data from public filings at www.sec.gov

Although it's impossible to assign improvement to each specific strategy employed, one can clearly see the growth in Gross Margin to respectable levels because 78% is the median Subscription Gross Margin among the broader comparable set of all SaaS companies. Dropbox completed its IPO on March 23, 2018. Following the strength of its fiscal year 2017 performance, including the dramatic Gross Margin improvement, Dropbox sold shares to the public at $29 per share. This share price implied an enterprise value of $9.2 billion, which equates to a respectable multiple of enterprise value to revenue of 8.3x.

Since its IPO, Dropbox continued to improve its Gross Margin, steadily increasing it to 80% for fiscal year 2021.

Dropbox's Operating margins illustrate how the high COR impacts the financial profile. The Research and Development and General and Administrative cost categories averaged 27% and 17% of revenue, respectively, for fiscal year 2015, by which time revenue was a hair over $600 million. These margins are consistent with those of SaaS companies broadly, especially those at these revenue levels when companies have achieved scale. Looking at two prominent B2C SaaS companies—Box and HubSpot—as specific comparable companies for the years with equivalent revenue levels, we can see that cost categories were consistent, with Research and Development at 23% and 27% and General and Administrative at 15% and 14%. However, Sales and Marketing expenses were only 29% versus 51% and 50% for Box and HubSpot. This begs the question, how did Dropbox grow at a 22% CAGR over the past five years with such a low level of Sales and Marketing expenses? The answer is that the cost of the Free Offering, which is the cost of the GTM strategy, is accounted for in COR and not in Sales and Marketing. We can normalize Dropbox's Sales and Marketing expenses margin by assuming a 75% gross margin and moving the remainder of the expenses into the Sales and Marketing cost category. Under this assumption, the Sales and Marketing expenses margin is 89%. This margin is high compared to those of Box and HubSpot but still consistent with high-growth SaaS companies. And it's for the year before the company made the operational changes described above. The point of this discussion is to reinforce the need to understand the mechanics of your comparable companies when using this type of analysis for decision making.

Dropbox's strong performance allowed it to achieve significant scale and to grow gross margin to 80% in fiscal year 2021. Note that the company did this while reducing Sales and Marketing expenses margin to 20%. This result represents strong business performance as can be seen in the RO40 metric. Dropbox achieved an RO40 metric of 46 (12% growth and 22% FCF) in fiscal year 2021.

Accounting for Free Offerings has changed recently. Increasingly, companies allocate direct costs associated with the Free Offerings—Freemium or Fee trials—to Sales and Marketing expenses. This accounting methodology provides investors with a more accurate representation of business performance. Similarly, for internal, this allocation helps decision makers in the same way.

Dropbox performs well on a cash flow basis due to the focus on up-front payments. In this way, the company avoids the Working Capital Trough problem we discussed earlier. Dropbox pricing offers a 17%–20% discount as an incentive for annual payments. Also, the pricing default is shown as annual payments; subscribers would have to switch to monthly payments for this cadence. The net result is that Dropbox generates positive working capital each period. We typically use FCF as a percentage of revenue for comparable analyses. But to illustrate the impact of up-front payments, we will use changes in working capital as a percentage of revenue. The change in working capital is defined as the period-to-period change in the net of current assets and current liabilities. For fiscal years 2017–2019, Dropbox generated positive working capital between $80,000 and $90,000 and this averages approximately 6% of revenue. By way of comparison, Box and HubSpot generated working capital at averages of 1% and 3%, respectively, for the same three years. So Dropbox outperforms its peers in generating working capital by its ability to collect up-front payments.

Dropbox was one of the first SaaS companies to highlight cohort performance. Dropbox's S-1 filing includes two charts showing data that all SaaS companies need to prepare as part of its reporting cadence. The first shows the monthly subscription amount for all quarterly cohorts over a five-year period. The second provides a more detailed view of dollar-based expansion, shown indexed to the initial ARPU, for three quarterly cohorts. The main takeaways are the consistent onboarding of new subscribers and the dollar-value expansion of the individual cohorts. Dropbox performs extremely well on both activities, and this makes the charts compelling.

Internally, cohort reporting provides valuable insights into customer behavior. Cohorts should always be defined by months and may be segmented further by product used or by customer size. By tracking end user monthly subscription value over time, you will identify the actions that lead to expansions. Product teams can use this information to drive user expansion. Marketing teams can identify the end user marketing activities that drive higher ARPU. Monthly onboarding will demonstrate the efficacy of funnel conversion, allowing fine-tuning of customer acquisition efforts. Marketing teams will run separate campaigns in the same period to observe conversion rates. Tracking the sets of subscribers that responded to each campaign over time can reveal the long-term effectiveness of these campaigns. Segmenting cohorts by marketing campaign provides insights beyond the view provided by marketing systems. By observing churned customers, you can identify potential triggers and then act to help subscribers at that moment. For financial reporting, monthly cohort tracking enables precise customer lifetime calculations and improved CLTV/CAC reporting.

Dropbox, Inc. (DBX)
Year Ended December 31

in $ Thousands	2017	2018	2019	2020	2021
Annual Recurring Revenue	N/A	$ 1,530,000	$1,820,000	$ 2,052,000	$ 2,261,000
Statement of Operations					
Revenue	$1,106,800	$ 1,391,700	$1,661,300	$ 1,913,900	$ 2,157,900
Cost of Revenue	$ 356,700	$ 347,700	$ 395,200	$ 397,500	$ 421,000
Gross Profit	$ 750,100	$ 1,044,000	$1,266,100	$ 1,516,400	$ 1,736,900
Operating Expenses:					
Research & Development	$ 287,200	$ 400,000	$ 514,500	$ 553,400	$ 565,800
Sales & Marketing	$ 280,300	$ 345,300	$ 391,900	$ 389,100	$ 402,500
General & Administrative	$ 131,700	$ 142,600	$ 179,000	$ 191,200	$ 175,800
Total Operating Expenses	$ 699,200	$ 887,900	$1,085,400	$ 1,133,700	$ 1,144,100
Operating Income (Loss)	$ 50,900	$ 156,100	$ 180,700	$ 382,700	$ 592,800
Free Cash Flow					
Net Cash Provided by Operating Activities	$ 528,500	$ 330,300	$ 425,400	$ 570,800	$ 729,800
Capital Expenditures	$ (23,900)	$ (633,800)	$ (320,000)	$ (80,100)	$ (22,100)
Free Cash Flow	$ 504,600	$ (303,500)	$ 105,400	$ 490,700	$ 707,700
Key Metrics					
Paying Users	11,000,000	12,700,000	14,300,000	15,480,000	16,790,000
ARPU	$ 111.91	$ 117.64	$ 123.07	$ 128.50	$ 133.73
Magic Number	N/A	N/A	0.84	0.59	0.54
Margins					
Gross Margin	68%	75%	76%	79%	80%
Research & Development	26%	29%	31%	29%	26%
Sales & Marketing	25%	25%	24%	20%	19%
General & Administrative	12%	10%	11%	10%	8%
Operating Income (Loss)	5%	11%	11%	20%	27%
Free Cash Flow	46%	-22%	6%	26%	33%

Source: www.sec.gov regulatory filings

Dropbox serves as an excellent B2C Saas company example due to its low ARPU and extensive use of the freemium go-to-market strategy. Please note that all cost centers are shown excluding share-based compensation.

The lesson on cohorts is that the SaaS professional needs to provide detailed cohort reporting segmented in a way that best helps product and marketing teams understand how to improve the customer journey. This detail must be summarized into high-level reporting that helps the management team, board of directors, and investors understand business performance.

At the highest level, this section provides an example of a B2C SaaS company, showing the financial profile and SaaS metrics. The important takeaway is the value you gain from a detailed understanding of comparable companies. You can compare the data and produce reports consistent with industry expectations. And an in-depth understanding of related companies adds credibility to business performance.

Key Takeaways

- B2C SaaS companies make extensive use of cohorts in calculating CLTV/CAC. The most common use of cohort reporting is to consolidate all new customers into a monthly cohort and then track monthly net retention for a period of up to eighteen months. Due to the variety of digital marketing channels, these companies also use a more fine-tuned approach by creating customer cohorts by channel. Another common approach is to measure net retention of a new customer cohort generated by a specific marketing campaign.

- The effectiveness of Free Offerings in generating revenue is monitored for conversion rates to paid users, the average amount of time before converting, and the level of user engagement while on the Free Offering. The costs associated with the Free Offerings need to be included in the CLTV/CAC ratio calculation.

- Dropbox, Inc. serves as a good example of a B2C SaaS company because its average ACV is less than $10,000, it uses a Free Offering to generate customer leads, and it offers a point solution, i.e., storage, that a new customer can self-provision. Dropbox achieved success in the high conversion rate of customers on Free Offerings to paid accounts, in growing revenue both through average ARPU expansion and through customer count, and minimizing the impact of the Working Capital Trough with up-front payments. This success is shown achieving an RO40 metric of 46.

Summary of B2C Models

B2C SaaS companies face unique challenges due to the dynamics of its target market, i.e., individual consumers and the low value add of products offered. Individual consumers are bombarded with lead-generation messages for B2C applications, and companies need to break through the marketing noise. Consumers are fickle and may churn for any number of micro and macro reasons. Barriers to entry are low, and this enables competitive threats from any mobile application developer. The low value add limits pricing power and results in low average ACV. The low average profit per customer requires sophisticated use of digital marketing channel strategies to maximize ROI. Unexpectedly, increases in metrics such as Churn or CPL can quickly create cash flow losses and sometimes before management realizes it. These dynamic challenges require a sophisticated business intelligence and finance team to effectively manage the unique risks.

Summary of Customer-Centric SaaS Models

The three types of Customer-Centric SaaS models each offer software subscriptions but use very different means of selling subscriptions to customers. These GTM strategies create different financial profiles and result in very different key performance metrics. Applying the customer-centric framework to your company will help you choose the best metrics for managing your business.

SaaS Business Model Comparison	Customer-Centric Category		
	Enterprise	SMM	B2C
Average Annual Contract Value	$50K+	$10K - $50K	<$10K
Services Revenue as % of Total	20%- 40%	10% - 20%	None
Average Sales Cycle	6 - 9 months	1-3 months	< 1 month
Dominant GTM Strategies	Direct/Channel	Indirect/Inbound	Freemium/ Free Trial
Product	Robust functionality and extensive integration	Light functionality and few integration points	Point solution
Service Delivery	High-Touch	Self-Serve	Self-Serve

Unique SaaS Metrics		Enterprise	SMM	B2C
	Top Line	Contracted Annual Recurring Revenue (CARR) Professional Services Attach Rate (PSAR)	Contracted Monthly Recurring Revenue (CMRR) Billings Cadence	Annual Recurring Revenue (ARR) Billings Cadence
	Go-to-Market	AE productivity Days to Close	Marketing Campaign ROI; Marketing Lead Conversion Rate	Marketing Campaign ROI; Free to Paid Conversion Rate
	Unit Economics	Sales Efficiency Customer Retention Expansion Rate	CLTV/CAC First Response Time; First Contact Response Rate; Escalation Rate End User Engagement	CLTV/CAC Daily Active Users to Monthly Active Users (DAU/MAU) User Retention by Time period

PART 3

INDUSTRY-CENTRIC MODELS

The Industry-Centric SaaS business model classification provides an alternative framework for evaluating SaaS companies. The Customer-Centric framework segments SaaS companies by the size of their customers. The Industry-Centric SaaS framework separates SaaS companies into two categories: those that develop software for a specific industry (vertical) versus those that develop software for a specific function regardless of industry (horizontal). Both frameworks are valuable tools for the SaaS professional. Gaining a full understanding of both frameworks will help you make the best recommendation on financial reporting, metric measurement, and management and strategic initiatives.

CHAPTER 15

HORIZONTAL SAAS MODELS

Overview

Company	Administrative Function
Avalera	Tax
Bill.com	Invoicing
Coupa	Procurement
Dropbox	Collaboration
HubSpot	Marketing
Slack	Collaboration
Smartsheet	Project Management
Workday	Human Resources
Xero	Accounting
Zendesk	Customer Service
Zoom	Collaboration

Horizontal SaaS companies typically start with basic administrative functions common to all companies. Salesforce is the most prominent Horizontal SaaS company; founded in 1999, it started with a management tool for Direct Sales teams. Hubspot was founded seven years later with an inbound marketing tool. ZenDesk built a customer service application for any company with a call center. Several companies built administrative applications for accounting (Xero), billing (Bill.com), sales tax calculations (Avalara), procurement (Coupa), human resource management (Workday), and project management (Smartsheet). Cloud-based software design lends itself to collaboration, and several applications were founded to take advantage of this instantaneous connection ability. Dropbox allows users to easily store and share documents online. The Slack messaging application's popularity is second only to email. Zoom brought video conferencing to the masses with its ridiculously easy software application. I list these companies and their application's functions in the image here. All make really good comparable companies for benchmarking.

When SaaS business models originated, the most successful venture-backed startups used a horizontal model. The reason behind the horizontal strategy was that it enabled the company to serve the largest possible market, i.e., TAM. The software functionality only needed to be very basic, so the Research and Development resource requirements were typically light. The targeted functions to be replicated in the software, e.g., customer databases and bookkeeping, were well defined. The emerging cloud infrastructure at the time best served simple services that required low bandwidth, computing, and storage capacities. Finally, perpetual software providers were slow to shift to a SaaS model because doing so would reduce revenue growth during the pivot. This opened the door to SaaS companies seeking to disrupt these entrenched competitors. These factors resonated well with the investment theses of venture capital firms.

As Horizontal SaaS companies mature, they add functionality to their base product and can even begin targeting other verticals. But the core product continues to address the basic administrative functionality.

Prominent Horizontal SaaS company examples include **Salesforce**, which makes Customer Relationship Management software in use by direct and Indirect Sales teams regardless of the product or service the team is selling; **Microsoft Office 365** productivity suite is the most widely used software of its category; **HubSpot's** marketing software is used by 86,000 companies in over 120 countries and this demonstrates its broad functionality; **Intuit's QuickBooks Online** software provides simple accounting and bookkeeping software in use by sole proprietor businesses to venture-backed technology startups and everything in between; **Zoom**, one of many office productivity applications, is in use by elementary schools, Fortune 1000 customers, and every size of company in between.

Financial Profile

Horizontal SaaS companies have low ACV offerings because the software is so basic. Over time, as these companies grew their market power and software functionality, they were able to push up price points. But even today, large entrenched market players have low-cost offerings. The four large horizontal product offerings mentioned above have ACVs that range from $72–$540 on a per-user basis. Zoom's basic plan is free.

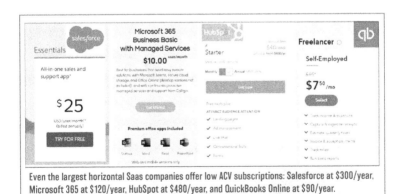

Even the largest horizontal Saas companies offer low ACV subscriptions: Salesforce at $300/year, Microsoft 365 at $120/year, HubSpot at $480/year, and QuickBooks Online at $90/year.

These low-cost options are very profitable because the cost to serve is extremely low and because basic, mature products require very little engineering support. Obviously, these players have built high value-added products by increasing the software functionality. High-end products command six- and seven-figure ACV pricing.

New Horizontal SaaS companies compete with even lower cost offerings hoping to capture market share and build their own high-value products. Using a Fast Follower strategy, several of these companies had considerable success. Online accounting software provider Xero was founded in 2006 and was the third most popular accounting software after QuickBooks and Intacct. Contrast this success with that of Intuit, which launched desktop app QuickBooks in 1998 and its online version two years before Xero's founding. Despite Intuit's lead, Xero grew faster than Intuit's Small Business Segment (products and subscriptions), outperforming the large competitor with a ten-year CAGR of 43% versus 3% for Intuit.

Revenue by Year, *in $Millions*	'12	'13	'14	'15	'16	'17	'18	'19	'20	'21
Intuit (note 1)	$811	$849	$851	$709	$709	$908	$1,038	$1,036	$1,032	$1,085
Xero	$19	$39	$67	$124	$202	$295	$407	$553	$718	$848

Source: Public filings. www.sec.gov for Intuit (INTU); www2.asx.com.au for Xero (XRO)

Note 1 Intuit financial information for Small Business segment revenue, which is derived primarily from QuickBooks Desktop software products, including QuickBooks Desktop Pro, QuickBooks Desktop Premier, QuickBooks Accountant Desktop, and QuickBooks Enterprise; QuickBooks Basic Payroll and QuickBooks Enhanced Payroll; QuickBooks Point of Sale solutions; ProAdvisor Program memberships for the accounting professionals who serve small businesses; and financial supplies

By the 2020s, the Horizontal SaaS space was fully mature and characterized by large competitors and commoditized offerings for every possible business and consumer function, leaving very few opportunities for new entrants. This high-growth phase of Horizontal SaaS had passed, and investors began moving to Vertical SaaS opportunities.

Key Takeaways

- Horizontal SaaS companies offer software that runs common business functions such as accounting, customer relationship management, marketing, and human resource management, among many others.

- This approach gives the company the opportunity to serve the largest potential market which we call TAM.

- These software offerings have low ACV because the product is so basic, but the business can still be profitable because Research and Development costs are low, end users require little support since many understand the administrative function, and because the SaaS model makes software delivery efficient.

- Once the early Horizontal SaaS companies gained success, new companies sprang up to focus on writing software to support increasingly niche business functions such as online surveys and performance reviews.

- Because the software is so basic, the barriers to entry are low. This market dynamic allows new entrants to introduce competitive software using fewer resources to achieve the same amount of revenue.

- Fast-Followers are new entrants that catch up to and even overtake market leaders. The accounting software company **Xero** is a good example. It launched a low-cost product that helped drive a high-growth revenue trajectory. Xero nearly overtook market leader Intuit's QuickBooks product within a nine-year period.

- Examples of successful Horizontal SaaS companies include **Salesforce, HubSpot, Microsoft 365, QuickBooks,** and **Zoom**. Studying such established companies' paths to success will help you launch a new competitive product.

CHAPTER 16

VERTICAL SAAS MODELS

Overview

Company	Industry
athenahealth	Medical
Dealertrack	Automotive
Demandware	E-commerce
Fleetmatics	Transportation
Opower	Electric utilities
Q2 Holdings	Banking
Textura	Commercial construction
Veeva	Life science & pharmaceutical
Guidewire	Property and casualty insurance
Instructure	Education
Real Page	Property management

Vertical SaaS companies develop software that is customized for a specific industry rather than a specific function. Such companies evolved much later than Horizontal SaaS companies, but both the number of Vertical SaaS companies and their revenues are growing faster. Today, we find numerous successful Vertical SaaS businesses, some of which are included in the nearby chart. The successful rise of Vertical SaaS led to the saying, "*There are riches in niches.*"

It's easy to understand why Vertical SaaS companies developed more slowly than did Horizontal SaaS companies. With a very focused software application, these companies have a limited TAM opportunity. The software development is much more resource intensive because digitizing specific industry functions is much more complex. The existing functions are customized to specific industry needs and are not well understood externally. Existing systems tend to be older and more unique, and this makes integrations more challenging. Many functions are subject to government regulations such as the healthcare privacy law HIPAA or the requirement for FDA approval of pharmaceutical advertisements. Some industries have entrenched, dominant market share competitors that may not be open to new technologies. Even if the interest/openness is there, the software procurement experience could not. Horizontal SaaS played a key role in educating customers and in building skillsets, and this took some time.

There was also a cultural issue that needed to be addressed before the development of Vertical SaaS could begin to take off. Success requires industry experience, and this requires collaboration between technology-minded entrepreneurs and industry experts. Early software entrepreneurs understand technology but not the processes, procedures, and requirements of specific industries. It was natural for them to start companies to digitize common administrative functions. Industry experts understand their business but often don't have the technology mindset. These people spent their careers learning the industry inside and out, and this journeyman trajectory did not include experience with the latest in cloud technologies. Thus, the entrepreneurs and the industry experts needed to find each other before Vertical SaaS companies could be built.

As the SaaS industry matured, these barriers fell away, opening the door to the rise of Vertical SaaS companies. Once they became established players, Vertical SaaS companies found that their business model had two main advantages.

High Sales Efficiency—Vertical SaaS companies gain unique experience selling into industry verticals and typically employ a "Land and Expand" GTM strategy. These factors drive higher sales efficiency than is found in Horizontal SaaS companies. A focus on vertical sales gives the software provider a detailed understanding of the optimum use case. Research and Development uses this information to tailor the product accordingly and this makes the sale easier. Customer case studies and customer references will help enable prospective customers to quickly grasp the value added and this, too, facilitates the sale. The "Land and Expand" strategy generates high sales efficiency following the initial contract because the cost to expand a customer is about half that to acquire a new customer. Plus, the payback period is materially shorter: estimated at 10%–30% shorter by the KeyBanc SaaS Survey.

Formidable Competitive Advantage—The complexity of software development combined with industry expertise created a deep moat around their business. The stronger a company's market position, the greater the pricing power. With reduced new entrant competitive threats, the incumbent Vertical SaaS player can raise prices to match the product's value added. Experience in serving customers allows the company to provide consultative services, proactively helping existing customers navigate challenges that are well documented and well understood inside the SaaS organization. This further demonstrates value added and, thus, supports pricing power.

Financial Profile

The Vertical SaaS business model sales efficiency can be seen in the data pulled from public filings via www.sec.gov. For this analysis, use Sales and Marketing expenses as a percentage of revenue as a proxy for sales efficiency. This is a variation on the definition presented earlier.

The below charts show Sales and Marketing expenses as a percentage of revenue for public Horizontal and Vertical SaaS companies for revenue tiers beginning at $25 million and increasing by $25 million increments through $300 million. This approach normalizes the data to account for scale, which increases sales efficiency as the company's revenues grow. The trendline is a logarithmic fit of the mean at each revenue tier. As an example, compare the two types of companies at $200 million in revenue. The Vertical SaaS company spends $40 million on Sales and Marketing; the Horizontal SaaS company spends nearly $60 million. This analysis shows the superior sales efficiency of the Vertical SaaS model.[2]

Vertical SaaS companies that achieve this superior sales efficiency can choose to invest more heavily in Research and Development or to pursue profitability or a combination thereof. Veeva Systems, a software platform for the life sciences and pharmaceutical industry, invests heavily in Research and Development with 21% of revenue allocated to Research and Development while spending 16% on Sales and Marketing. Guidewire, a software platform used by property and casualty insurers, spends 26% of revenue on Research and Development and 20% on Sales and Marketing. Research and Development expenses are not consistently higher than Sales and Marketing expenses across all Vertical SaaS companies, but it's always higher relative to that of Horizontal SaaS companies.

Vertical SaaS Example: Veeva Systems

There are several Horizontal SaaS companies that you can use as comparables for benchmarking. All of the examples shown in Part 2, the Customer-Centric SaaS Model, are horizontally focused companies. So Chapter 16 ends with a high-profile public company example. Veeva Systems, Inc. is a Vertical SaaS company in

---

2   Tomaz Tunguz looked at this topic in his article, "Do Vertical SaaS Companies Benefit from Higher Sales Efficiency?" posted September 27, 2015. I believe that my more current analysis validates my assertion, but you can read Mr. Tunguz's article at https://tomtunguz.com/sales-efficiency-vertical-horizontal-gtm/.

Sales Efficiency- Horizontal vs Vertical Saas

S&M as % of Revenue over a Revenue Range from $25M to $300M

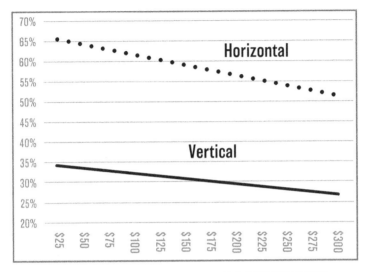

Vertical comps: VEEV, DWRE, OPWR, FLTX, TXTR, TRAK, QTWO, GWRE, INST, RP, ATH N.

Horizontal comps: ZOOM, WDAY, COUP, HU BS, ZEN, PLAN, AVLR, TENB, CRWD, QLYS, RPO, ZS

that it serves the life sciences and pharmaceutical industries. The software platform speeds the product life cycle by automating product development and the process that brings the products to market, all while ensuring government regulation compliance.

Veeva Systems' revenue growth trajectory is best-in-class for a Vertical SaaS company. It achieved a 46% CAGR over the fiscal periods from 2010 to 2022.

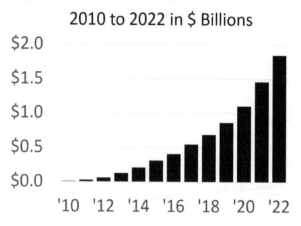

Veeva Systems, Inc. Growth Trajectory
2010 to 2022 in $ Billions

The growth trajectory lags T2D3 because Veeva Systems used services to augment the software platform. In 2010, the revenue mix was 52% SaaS and 48% services. This revenue mix is common among early-stage Vertical SaaS companies because the software is new and still requires a lot of technical and advisory support. Often, the company operates their own software on behalf of the customer because the customer does not have the internal expertise. As the business progresses, the company continues to enhance the software by automating service features. And customers begin bringing the work inside and staffing teams to run the software. Thus, the revenue mix shifts over time. Veeva Systems achieved an 80%/20% SaaS to services revenue mix by 2017 and has maintained it through fiscal year 2022.

Veeva Systems earned an 85% Gross Margin on its SaaS business in fiscal year 2022. This rate is higher than the median benchmark of 78% and likely reflects pricing power since it is the market leader in this vertical. The services business earns a Gross Margin of about 22% on average over the past five years. This result is on the low end of the 20%–40% we expect, but this low-end rate could imply that the company prices services revenue lower in exchange for higher SaaS margin. Since SaaS revenue is recurring, the increase in CLTV likely more than offsets the lower services business margin.

Veeva Systems, Inc.	2018	2019	2020	2021	2022
Revenues:					
Subscription	$559	$ 694	$ 896	$ 1,179	$ 1,484
Professional	131	168	208	286	367
Total revenues	691	862	1,104	1,465	1,851
Cost of revenues	211	245	303	409	504
Gross profit	479	617	801	1,056	1,347
Gross margin	69%	72%	73%	72%	73%
Operating expenses (OpEx)					
R&D	132	159	210	294	382
S&M	129	149	190	235	288
G&A	60	86	114	149	172
Total OpEx	321	394	514	678	842
Operating income	158	223	286	378	505
Free Cash Flow	233	311	136	171	337
Key Metrics					
Customer count	625	719	861	993	1,205
ARPA	$895	$ 966	$ 1,041	$ 1,188	$ 1,232
Revenue Retention	121%	122%	121%	124%	119%
Operating Margins:					
R&D	19%	18%	19%	20%	21%
S&M	19%	17%	17%	16%	16%
G&A	9%	10%	10%	10%	9%
Total OpEx	47%	46%	47%	46%	45%
Free Cash Flow	34%	36%	12%	12%	18%

Notes: (a) for fiscal years ending January 31; (b) in dollar millions
Source: www.sec.gov

You will notice how Research and Development expenses grow as a percentage of revenue even with the strong revenue growth over the past five years. Sales and Marketing expenses decline over the same period. We discussed how Vertical SaaS companies achieve higher sales efficiency above. The continued decline of

Sales and Marketing expenses implies that the company's status as market leader requires a lower investment in this area.

Veeva Systems has generated positive EBITDA and FCF continuously since fiscal year 2014, the first year these figures are available. This is also a result consistent with Vertical SaaS company performance because the software adds more value to the vertical than does a Horizontal SaaS company to the broader economy.

The average customer ACV, shown here as "Average Subscription Revenue per Customer," demonstrates that Veeva Systems is a true Enterprise SaaS company. The lesson in this is that the two classifications introduced in this book cannot be considered separately. Any given SaaS company will demonstrate characteristics of the two classifications.

Key Takeaways

- Vertical SaaS companies offer software that is tailored to a specific industry rather than a specific function.

- Vertical SaaS companies were typically founded after Horizontal SaaS companies because the software complexity is high and the target market is small.

- Many Vertical SaaS companies were founded by industry operators who recognized a niche opportunity and built productivity software to address the specific problem.

- Companies that operate a vertical strategy can achieve high sales efficiency because the use case is well defined and the software is built specifically for this purpose. The product itself drives the sales motion.

- Once established, Vertical SaaS companies' experience in the industry serves as a formidable competitive advantage, and this raises the barriers to entry.

- Vertical and Horizontal SaaS companies' financial profiles differ in that the former has higher sales efficiency as measured by Sales and Marketing expenses as a percentage of revenue and this frees up cash flow for investments in Research and Development or to improve cash flow.

- Veeva Systems serves as a good Vertical SaaS comparable company due to its high SaaS Gross Margin, its sales efficiency, and its profitability. And its history of moving toward a higher mix of SaaS to services revenue is common to that of many Vertical SaaS companies.

SUMMARY

Congratulations on completing the study of my book. You gained an understanding of business and SaaS management that took me more than two decades to earn. We walked through a framework for thinking about SaaS management and reviewed the most important metrics for each category of business. Before we finish up, let's review some challenges that I have experienced. I invite you now to think through your actions in such scenarios.

An Enterprise SaaS company was founded with a transaction-based business model. Per-transaction pricing matched the value add that the customer gained from the platform; customers only paid for what they used. The company decided to pivot to a SaaS model to gain better traction with the investor community. The CEO described the unique challenge in executing the pivot: "We didn't really know what SaaS was, so we just made it up as we went along." This subset of the management team described the struggle with invoicing, sales commission planning, SaaS metrics management, budgeting, and reporting. The CRO described reading blog posts to get a better understanding of SaaS.

- If you were in my shoes during this discussion, what questions would you ask the participants to better understand the operating strategy?

- What would be your next steps in evaluating the success of their SaaS pivot?

- How would you advise the company on product development and organizational design to maximize the probability of success as a SaaS business?

- What performance metrics would you introduce?

- How would you train the management on the SaaS business model?

A B2C SaaS company achieves product market fit. By testing multiple marketing channels, the company identifies two specific channels that both produce a strong CLTV/CAC ratio. The company begins a significant digital marketing campaign to generate online leads. Marketing spend increases by a multiple of ten over prior periods.

- How would you best be able to play a strategic role in the company?

- Think about the problems you would expect the company to encounter going forward with this strategy. What metrics would you implement to give advance warning of any problems?

- How would you prepare the management team for such challenges?

An Enterprise SaaS company has a 64% consolidated gross margin. It earns 40% gross margin on professional services, which makes up 30% of total revenue. Onboarding takes only six weeks, Customer Success delivers end user engagement and DBNR is 140%. The RO40 is 56. However, CLTV/CAC is just 0.8x. The company's fundraising has been difficult, and the company is under financial pressure.

- How would you think about evaluating the company's strategy?

- What metrics would you use to validate your hypothesis?

- How could you get the fundraising back on track?

A large public company sells a combined hardware and software product. The company has been the market leader for many years. However, Revenues and Gross Margin have been declining because the hardware is becoming a commoditized product. Competitors that entered this market only a few years ago sell SaaS products that perform many of the same functions.

- How would you advise the company on transitioning to a SaaS business model?

- What new metrics would you introduce to stakeholders?

- How would you gain the credibility to present a compelling strategic plan?

An SMM SaaS company has increased its product stability and functionality. The average ACV has increased accordingly and is now above $20,000. The CLTV/CAC is 3.5x based on this higher ACV and a sales efficiency due to a strong inside sales team. The company believes that it can sell to Fortune 1000 companies. The CEO needs advice on product pricing and the GTM strategy.

- What data would you need to create a recommendation?

- What other business changes should you recommend?

- How would you evaluate funding strategies?

A big data company sells perpetual software that customers download and run in their own data centers. The on-premise software is usually required because the amount of data is too large to be moved over the internet. The product is the best in the business. The CEO wants to become a SaaS company and asks if the accounting can be changed to represent the company as having a SaaS business model.

- What would be your initial response?

- What would you need to know about the product before providing guidance?

- How would you devise a strategic plan for changing the business model?

The board of an Enterprise SaaS company requires the company to maintain an RO40 metric above 40. Annual budgets are built around this concept. The company has grown to over $300 million in total revenue, but year-over-year growth is slowing. In the current budget cycle, the forecasted RO40 for the next fiscal year is projected to fall short of this metric. It seems that the company can only operate by restructuring the business or operating below the RO40.

- How would you evaluate each option?

- What information would you need to collect for your analysis?

- How would you incorporate benchmarking into the process?

- How do you gain credibility for your ultimate recommendation?

Now that you've read the book, I hope that you will be up for such challenges. This is the true purpose for writing the book. I wanted to write a book that consolidates all of the knowledge gained from a career working with SaaS companies into one resource. Anyone who wants to learn the business can do so by studying this book and merging the concepts with their experience working in SaaS companies. Thus, I dedicate this book to these motivated individuals who start their SaaS careers with this knowledge and who will take part in driving the next wave of innovation in the SaaS business.

ACKNOWLEDGMENTS

I'd like to start by thanking my colleagues at FLG Partners where I have worked for these past five years. Our Managing Partner, Laureen Debuono, serves as a constant source of inspiration and mentorship to me and everyone at the firm. Through her leadership, Laureen has grown the partnership's bench strength, adding experienced partners who have grown our brand exponentially. Our Administrative Partner, Heather Ogan, keeps the entire firm organized and who implemented a structure that allows us to scale our team. Among the partners, I would like to thank Stephanie Roberts and Bill Beyer, who became partners at the same time as I; as the 2017 cohort, we stay close and share ideas and also have fun dinners. Fuad Ahmad and I became friends through FLG Partners and shared time at work and with our families. Greg Curhan is one of the most experienced transaction CFOs and has been involved in some of our largest fundraisings. I email him whenever I have transaction-related questions. SaaS heavyweights Ron Fior and Ken Chow graciously gave up several weekends to review and provide feedback on my manuscript. I wrote about two-thirds of the manuscript in the form of articles I posted to the FLG blog, *FLG Perspectives*. One of the FLG Partners founders and former Managing Partner Jeffrey Kuhn reviewed each and every one of these articles and gave me the type of feedback that helped me produce better articles as I continued to write.

I would like to thank two SaaS influencers who helped define the SaaS business model and advance innovation in this business. Lauren Kelley is founder and CEO of OPEXEngine, the world's largest SaaS company benchmarking database. Lauren is a true visionary in that she founded OPEXEngine in 2006 and shepherded the business through all the ups and downs of the industry since then. OPEXEngine is the go-to benchmarking product for SaaS CFOs managing the budgeting process, the reporting cadence, and the unfortunate restructuring. The data allows CFOs to serve as true business partners to their management teams and strategic thinkers for their companies. OPEXEngine is now becoming a standard for SaaS portfolio tracking and benchmarking for private equity firms investing in SaaS. Lauren continues to serve as a leader in the SaaS business and is a founding member of the SaaS Metrics Board, an open source organization dedicated to helping the industry adopt standard definitions and usage of SaaS metrics. You can learn more at https://www.opexengine.com/.

David Spitz is equally as important a SaaS influencer who founded the Pacific Crest SaaS Survey (now the KeyBanc SaaS Survey) and authored this report for over a decade. This annual publication served as go-to study for SaaS metric definitions and benchmarks. A whole generation of SaaS operators learned the basics from his work. David founded BenchSights, which offers benchmarking software (SaaS, of course) for GTM strategies. He now has extensive experience in helping SaaS CROs and RevOps teams optimize revenue performance with benchmarking. CFOs use BenchSights to help them serve as business partners. You can learn more at https://benchsights.com/.

A special thanks to Erik Suppiger, Sr. Research Analyst–Internet Networking and Security Equipment at JMP Securities. I first met Erik in 2006 when I started my first public company CFO role and Erik was one of our equity analysts. We stayed in touch over the past fifteen years and have shared thoughts on industry trends throughout that time. Erik also participated as a panel guest for my webinar on SaaS Pivots. Erik's insights into public equity research have helped shape my thinking on the business of SaaS.

I need to thank Jim DeBlasio, CFO and EVP of Operations at KeyFactor, for all the guidance and mentorship he provided to me over the past decade and a half. He has served as CEO and CFO in public and private companies in a career spanning over three decades.

One of my favorite CFOs and the most experienced cybersecurity CFO in that industry, Terry Murphy, and I met when I was interim CFO at a company called Kenna Security. He took over from me and took the company to new heights. Terry graciously helped with review and feedback on the book. Thanks, Terry!

I would like to thank my good friend Phil Kaplan, who hired me in my first public company CFO role at the company he founded, VitalStream, Inc. Later, we co-founded a virtual private cloud company called DemandFlex to bring the power of the private clouds to companies of all sizes. Our timing was not great, having started the company on the eve of the Great Recession. Phil continues to serve as a mentor and, more importantly, is a close friend of my family.

I need to thank the Scribe team, who collectively added such tremendous value to my book. Lily Wood made the first contact and stood by me every step of the way. AJ Hendrickson, my editor, gave my manuscript all the trappings of a real business book. She's an experienced editor of over 1,000 business books and articles. Aspiring business book authors would be remiss to use another editor as she is the best in the business. The book cover originated with a phenomenal design created by my daughter, Alexis Mersch. I thank Lindsey Bailey, Cover Designer and Graphic Designer at Scribe, for turning my daughter's vision into an elegant business book cover.

This section would not be complete without a big thank-you to my family. I'm grateful to my wife, Andi Trindle Mersch, who picked up far more of the family duties during the time I took off to write the manuscript, despite her own job as VP, Operations and Sustainability at Philz Coffee. My daughter, Alexis, who inspired me with her engagement in the process. She listened in on my calls with Lilly, AJ, and Lindsey and developed the first cover concept. Alexis also keeps asking about my next book. And my son, Nicholas, who joked that I wrote the book to feel good about myself. Well, it certainly did that, son!

ABOUT THE AUTHOR

Eric Mersch has over twenty years of executive finance experience including twice serving in public company Chief Financial Officer roles. Eric is an equity partner at FLG Partners where he works as an Interim CFO to venture-backed SaaS and subscription companies, specializing in Strategy and Operations, Strategic Planning, Equity and Debt Fundraising, Financial Planning and Analysis, Business Intelligence, and Accounting and Control. He's worked with SaaS companies in the big data, cybersecurity, internet infrastructure, advertising/marketing technology, mobile application, real estate technology, hospitality technology, and payment processing spaces. He is an expert in Go-To-Market strategies for Enterprise SaaS companies.

Earlier in his career, he served as Chief Financial Officer, Chief Accounting Officer, and VP, HR for ZipRealty, a publicly listed, real estate technology company. In this role, he joined the management team in the dramatic turnaround and successful sale of the business to real estate conglomerate Realogy Holdings Corp (NYSE:RLGY) in 2014. While at ZipRealty, Eric played a key role in reorganizing corporate overhead, developing a new Go-To-Market strategy and launching a new SaaS product. In his first public company role, he served as Chief Financial Officer for VitalStream (NASDAQ:VSTH), a Content Distribution Network (CDN) company, providing data storage and streaming services for digital media companies. He introduced unit economic analysis and drove significant efficiencies in LTV/CAC. He managed due diligence in the company's successful sale to Internap.

He also worked at Caesars Entertainment as Director Corporate Planning and later as VP, Finance for the Harrah's and Flamingo Resorts, an $800-million revenue business. Prior to his civilian career, Eric served in the US Navy as a submarine officer on the USS *Los Angeles*.

Eric holds an MBA from Harvard Business School and a bachelor of science in economics from the US Naval Academy and is a graduate of the US Navy's Nuclear Power School.

Eric continues to write about the SaaS business model in articles posted at the FLG Partners' website, www.flgpartners.com, under *FLG Perspectives*. He can be reached at emersch@flgpartners.com.

SAAS GLOSSARY

A

Annual Contract Value (ACV)—The annual value of a customer's Subscription Revenue only. It does not include non-recurring activities. The SaaS business model relies on Subscription Revenue because it is recurring revenue delivered at a very high gross margin. Providing software as a service generates value for the company over a much longer period than does perpetual software. This is the main value of the SaaS model; therefore, nearly all SaaS metrics use Subscription-related terms. Recurring revenue such as maintenance and customer support should not be included in the Subscription Revenue ACV; these are low-margin activities that do not add significant value to the business model. A variation of ACV is **Total Contract Value (TCV)**, which is the total value of the contract's Subscription Revenue measured over the life of the contract regardless of the Billings terms. As an example, a two-year contract has a TCV that is twice the amount of its ACV. Billing terms do not impact the TCV. In this two-year contract example, Billing terms can require an up-front payment for the first year or an up-front payment for the two years. Regardless, the TCV will be the same in both scenarios. Note that the calculation may change slightly if the contract includes annual price increases. If, in our example, the price for the second year of the contract increases by 20%, then the TCV will be 2.2x the ACV. For reporting purposes, a useful metric is the ratio of TCV to ACV. The higher the ratio, the "stickier" the customer base, leading to retention improvements and a more efficient sales cycle.

Annual Recurring Revenue (ARR)—The Subscription Revenue of a given period expressed as an annual run rate for all contracts with Revenue Recognition Dates prior to the period close date. ARR differs from CARR mainly due to the time it takes to onboard a customer. Additionally, the customer may want the contract to start on some specific future date. Finally, contracts with start dates after the first of the month are prorated for the number of days active in that month. A variation of ARR is **Contracted Annual Recurring Revenue (CARR),** which is the Subscription Revenue of a given period calculated as an annual run rate for all contracts including those that were signed in the same period. CARR differs from ARR for two main reasons. First, CARR includes the ARR of new customers that are not yet live because the customer onboarding process is not yet complete. The time it takes to get the customer live (Time to Live, or TTL) is a function of the company's ability to onboard new customers efficiently, but the customer's preparedness and commitment may drive a delay as well. So TTL is not entirely within the company's control. This dynamic makes CARR a more accurate KPI for Subscription Recurring Revenue. Second, using CARR avoids the step function changes in ARR. These changes are driven by the TTL in that revenue cannot be recognized until the customer is live, the date of which is referred to as the Go Live, thus meeting the GAAP/IFRS revenue recognition criteria for delivery. The contract will not generate revenue until the period of the Go Live date and will accumulate in deferred revenue during this time. Then, in the period of the Go Live date, all of the deferred revenue for this contract will be booked and this will increase the monthly subscription revenue for this customer by the number of months of deferred revenue. In the subsequent period, revenue will drop back down to the monthly subscription revenue. As an example, a new customer with a $120,000 ACV contract, which requires a three-month TTL, will have a monthly revenue pattern of zero for the first three months, $40,000 in the fourth month, and $10,000 in the fifth month and all subsequent months. This dynamic introduces volatility into the ARR metric. This is why CARR is the preferred metric for Enterprise SaaS companies. A monthly variation, **Committed Monthly Recurring Revenue (CMRR),** is the MRR that is under a contract term greater than one month. Put another way, all MRR under quarterly or annual contracts is referred to as CMRR. Contracts under longer terms have longer customer lifetimes and this makes such customers more valuable. CMRR is a common metric for SMM and B2C companies because they typically offer a mix of monthly, quarterly, and annual contracts, unlike Enterprise SaaS companies for which annual contracts are standard. CMRR and MRR are reported together, sometimes just with CMRR as a percentage of total MRR, and the difference between the two provides insight into the stability of the consumer base. For example, a company with 80% CMRR to total MRR has a more stable consumer base than one with 20% because fewer customers can churn in any given month.

ARR to End User (AEU) or MRR to End User (MEU)— Enterprise SaaS companies use this metric to evaluate the value added of their service if the pricing is based on end user count. The calculation is simply the ARR or MRR divided by the active end user count. If a service is properly priced, the price per user seat will tell you the true cost of your solution for your customer. The greater the number of active end users, the lower the cost per seat for the customer and this indicates a higher degree of engagement and a higher value added. Take special care in defining an active user as one would when doing so for the DAU/MAU calculation.

Average Days to Close—The average number of days for Marketing-Qualified Leads to convert to Bookings. This period of time is also referred to as the Contact-to-Close cycle.

B

Billings—The dollar value of the New or Renewal Subscription Bookings amount invoiced on the date defined by the contract terms, i.e., the Billings Date. In Enterprise SaaS companies with a high Average Selling Price, the Billing Date typically starts on the first of the month following the month of the Bookings Date but also may be delayed for several months while the customer waits on new budget dollars from a subsequent fiscal year or has tied payment to certain milestones. In B2C SaaS companies, the Billings Date is usually the date that the customer provisions the product by registering and entering a credit card number.

Bookings

> **Subscription Bookings**—At the highest level, the Subscription Bookings metric is defined as the ACV of a contract's Subscription Revenue. We use annual values because all GTM benchmarks are expressed in annual values. Plus, industry professionals, whether they are investors or operators, view the company's metrics on an annual basis. Another reason is that operators manage the business on an annual time period. Budgets are created for a given fiscal year. Sales Incentive Plans (SIPs) are based on annual quotas and annual attainment milestones for payments. We report on Subscription Bookings separate from all other

revenue streams because this revenue is the most critical to the success of the business.

Recurring Bookings—This is a term for the ACV of all recurring product and services contracts. Subscription Bookings are always recurring although contracts with less than one-year terms should be disclosed. An example of this is a pilot subscription. Recurring services bookings include Maintenance and Support revenue if the company is required to provide such services throughout the contract term. The adoption of ASC 606 creates a unique reporting situation for one-time professional services related to on-boarding a new customer, such as implementation and integration, software and business process customization, and training and enablement. Under ASC 606, these services are capitalized and amortized over the expected customer lifetime and this turns Professional Services bookings into recurring revenue. However, this is a GAAP requirement and is not relevant to SaaS reporting. CFOs should still report Professional Services Bookings as Non-Recurring Bookings.

Non-Recurring Bookings—This is the dollar value of all contracts for non-recurring revenue, which includes professional services, perpetual software license sales, and hardware sales. Enterprise SaaS companies offer complex software platforms, which typically require professional services for software implementation and training. These services are priced based on professional service hours performed. Since these are one-time offerings, we consider them to be non-recurring. Cybersecurity company CrowdStrike serves as a good example. This company reports both subscription, i.e., recurring, and professional services, i.e., non-recurring.

Companies pivoting to a SaaS business model will report subscription software and perpetual license software sales separately. For example, Development Operations, or DevOps, Platform provider JFrog uses two financial reporting categories for revenue: *Subscription-self-managed and SaaS* and *License-self-managed.* The second category refers to revenue derived from the sale of perpetual software licenses.

Nutanix, a provider of software solutions and cloud services that enable enterprise infrastructure, has three non-recurring revenue line items. Nutanix sells perpetual software licenses under the revenue title of "Non-Portable Software Revenue." The company also sells hardware and professional services. Nutanix is near the end of its pivot to SaaS with fiscal year 2022 perpetual license revenue at only 5% of total revenue versus 47% in fiscal year 2018.

Total Subscription Bookings—The ACV of both New Subscription Bookings and Renewal Subscription Bookings. We report these two Bookings types separately because Renewal Bookings are generally much less expensive to achieve than are New Subscription Bookings. In my experience, the CAC of Renewal Bookings can be as low as one-fifth that of New Bookings.

New Subscription Bookings—The ACV of both New Customer Subscription Bookings and Expansion Subscription Bookings as measured on the contract signature date, i.e., the Bookings Date. Best-in-class SaaS companies increase subscription revenue in two ways. The first is by adding new customers. The second is by selling more software subscriptions to existing customers. Thus, New Subscription Bookings must include both.

New Customer Subscription Bookings—The ACV of bookings from new customers acquired by the business as measured on the contract signature date. New customers are often referred to as "New Logos," meaning that the new customers have not had a prior relationship with your company. New customers may expand the dollar value of their original ACV soon after the initial purchase. When the expansion occurs within the same quarter of the original Booking (as defined by the contract date), the incremental ACV is typically referred to as "Fast-Follow Subscription Bookings" and this ACV is included as New Customer Subscription Bookings.

Expansion Subscription Bookings—The ACV of new subscriptions sold to an existing customer. Expansion Subscription Bookings are classified as either Upsell or Cross-Sell Bookings.

Upsell Subscription Bookings—The ACV of contracts that increase an existing customer's utilization of the original product. Adding more seat licenses or moving a customer to a higher usage tier are examples of Upsell Bookings.

Cross-Sell Subscription Bookings—The ACV of contracts that result in the sale of related or complementary software or service subscriptions to an existing customer.

Fast-Follow Subscription Bookings—The ACV of a Subscription Booking for an existing customer and that occurs in the same quarter as that of the initial contract date. Fast-Follow Bookings count as New Bookings for the purpose of sales commission calculations and quota retirement.

Renewal Subscription Bookings—The ACV of contract renewals measured at the Renewal Date, i.e., the date of term renewal regardless of the signature date. For example, a one-year contract with a signature date of 3/15/2022 and a start date of 4/1/2022 will have a renewal date of 3/31/2023. The contract can be renewed at any point before (preferably not after) the renewal date. But as long as the start date for the second year of the contract is 3/31/2023, Renewal Subscription Bookings are deemed to occur on this date. I also picked this example to illustrate a Renewal Date that lies in a separate quarter from the start date. In this case, the Renewal Bookings will occur in the first quarter (assuming the company's fiscal year follows the calendar year). The ACV of the Renewal Subscription Bookings will be the same as that of the original Subscription Bookings. Any increase in ACV for the subsequent year, or years, should be considered Expansion Bookings. This is true even if the original contract includes a price increase.

Reactivation Subscription Bookings—The ACV of Bookings from a prior customer that churned and was subsequently reacquired in a future period. This metric is commonly used in B2C companies that experience high churn due to low switching costs and serve a highly fragmented market. Such companies run marketing campaigns focused on churned users with specific reactivation incentives based on the consumers' behavior as an active customer. Reactivated consumers are tracked as a separate cohort within the company's revenue steam. This metric is typically expressed as MRR when used for this purpose. Enterprise SaaS companies will refer to Reactivation Subscription Bookings as New Subscription Bookings.

Available Bookings/Exposed Bookings—The Annual Recurring Revenue of all contracts up for renewal in a given period. This ARR is at risk of renewal and therefore is exposed to churning. Another version of this metric is the term(s) Available ACV or Available ARR. Companies with a high mix of Expansion to New Bookings use these terms to describe the upside available by expanding customers at the renewal date.

Buyer Type—The term "Buyer Type" refers to the specific role and level of the decision maker(s) who work for a potential customer.

C

Capital Consumption Ratio—I first encountered this metric in the KeyBanc Capital Markets, KBCM, (formerly Pacific Crest) SaaS Survey. The author and founder, David Spitz, defines it as the total capital consumed, both equity and debt, to date divided by the ARR achieved at that date. Expressed as a formula, this gives:

$$\text{Capital Consumption Ratio} = \frac{\text{Total Capital Consumed}}{\text{ARR Achieved}}$$

It is essentially a way to track progress toward profitability and is most useful for late-stage companies as they attain scale and approach profitability. You can see this use case in the KBCM survey data. The Capital Consumption Ratio shows a steady median ratio of 1.5x for companies with as little as $5 million in ARR all the way to $75 million. Additionally, the variance around the median declines as the ARR approaches $75 million indicating that this metric does not provide an effective benchmark for companies with ARR less than $75 million. The metric drops sharply to less than 1.0 for companies with ARR above $75 million and this trend evidences scale in the business.

Bessemer Venture Partners (BVP) created a metric called the **Cash Conversion Score**, or **CCS**, which is the inverse of the Capital Consumption Ratio. BVP uses a framework called the Good, Better, Best Framework for Cash Conversion Score. In this framework, BVP rates a portfolio company as Good if the CCS is in the 0.25x–0.5x range (this implies an IRR of 40%). The Better range is 0.5x–1.0x and this implies an IRR of 80%. The Best category includes any company performance above 1.0x and this implies an IRR of approximately 120%.

Channel Conflict—This term refers to any number of problems that arise when sales teams from two partner companies sell to the same target customer. Lack of coordination between the sales teams can lead to pricing, product, and brand confusion. Close cooperation may preclude your company from taking advantage of sales opportunities that conflict with the partnership agreement.

Conversion Rates

Free-to-Paid Conversion Rate—Used in companies with a Freemium or Free-Trial GTM strategy, the Free-to-Paid Conversion Rate is measured over time as the percentage of Freemium users that convert to paid subscriptions and at a point in time as the percentage of converted users divided by the total user population.

MQL-to-SAL Conversion Rate—Tracking the MQL-to-SAL conversion rates reveals insights into the sales cycle process. The MQL-to-SAL conversion rate is typically a function of the marketing team's ability to target prospective customers. Highly relevant marketing campaigns will drive the prospective customers with a high intent to purchase and this will lead to high conversion rates. A low conversion rate may have one or more of the following causes: Low rates may indicate that the MQLs do not fit with the Ideal Customer Profile; the SDR may uncover information that was not readily apparent from the MQL information envelope. Another potential reason is a disconnect in the understanding of the Ideal Customer Profile definition between sales and marketing.

Timing also plays a role. Companies with a long Sales Cycle will only benefit from tracking conversion rates over time; tracking monthly rates will likely show volatility. Companies that serve early markets will find that MQL-to-SAL conversion rates will lag benchmarks as they build brand awareness and educate the market. In this situation as well, tacking conversion rates over time makes more sense than looking at performance in individual months.

SAL-to-SQL Conversion Rate—Tracking this conversion rate metric is just as important. This conversion rate depends heavily on the specific SDR whose personality and sales skills are as important as the level of the SDR's training on the product, use case, and competition. The number of SQLs generated per period of time is often a performance objective and is used for the basis of incentive programs such as Management by Objective bonuses (MBOs). Outside of the specific SDR, the specific conversion rate is also influenced by the individual contact person at the company. Being able to identify the employees with purchasing authority is key to ensuring that the lead converts to a SQL. Without the right contacts, the AE will ask the SDR to continue building the relationship and networking to reach the right people.

One quick note on the MQL to SAL to SQL process: High-priority leads, colloquially called "hot leads," are routed directly to the AE and thereby skip qualification.

Customer Acquisition Cost (CAC)—The CAC is the average cost to acquire a new customer and is calculated as the Sales and Marketing expenses in a given period divided by New Customers acquired in the same period.

$$\text{CAC Ratio} = \frac{\text{Sales and Marketing Expense}}{\text{New Customers Acquired}}$$

When calculating CAC for an Enterprise SaaS company, the Bookings number should be matched with the associated Sales and Marketing expenses to the extent it is a practical exercise. Typically, Enterprise SaaS companies match Sales and Marketing expenses and the new customer count from the same year since variations in the Sales Cycles makes attribution difficult and, usually, not very valuable (see Sales Efficiency). SMM SaaS companies typically use the prior quarter or month since the sales cycle is shorter for these businesses. B2C SaaS companies typically use the prior month's Sales and Marketing expenses because the GTM strategy focuses on Call-to-Action marketing, which leads to a quick customer response. The CAC Ratio can be interpreted as the Sales and Marketing investment needed to acquire $1 of new Subscription Bookings.

Best practice for SaaS companies is to segment the CAC Ratio into two different ratios according to the type of sales activity defined as New Customer and Expansion. In my experience, the CAC for Expansion Bookings is approximately one-third the cost of acquiring New Customers. Therefore, distinguishing the CAC for each type of sale aids GTM strategy and management. When you use these specific measures, also provide a Blended CAC Ratio, which is the aggregate calculation for the business.

Customer Acquisition Cost (CAC) Ratio–Payback Period—The CAC Payback Period is the number of months required to pay back the associated customer acquisition costs and is calculated as the CAC divided by the Average Monthly Gross Profit.

Customer Lifetime Value (CLTV or LTV)—The average Net Present Value of the company's customers as defined by the Average Monthly Gross Profit multiplied by Customer Lifetime.

Customer Lifetime Value CLTV = ARPA x Gross Margin x Customer Lifetime

Where ARPA is the Average Revenue per Account (also referred to as ARPU or Average Revenue per Unit) as defined by the Average ARR of the customer base, GM is the Subscription Revenue Gross Margin, and Customer Lifetime is the average tenure of a customer and is calculated as the inverse of churn rate for mature SaaS companies but often set at between three and five years for early-stage companies.

Customer Lifetime Value to Customer Acquisition Cost (CLTV to CAC; LTV/CAC)—The CLTV/CAC ratio is a SaaS metric used to measure a company's sales efficiency using the relationship between the lifetime value of an average customer and the average cost of acquiring that customer. The metric, computed by dividing LTV by CAC, is a signal of customer profitability and of sales and marketing efficiency. A ratio greater than 1.0 implies that the company is generating value. Inversely, a ratio below 1.0 implies that the company is destroying value. Investors' expectations are that the CLTV/CAC ratio should fall within the 0.8–1.3 range with a clear path to achieving a ratio above 3.0x. However, the top-performing companies achieve 3.0x–5.0x.

$$CLTV/CAC = \frac{ARPA \times Gross\ Margin \times Customer\ Lifetime}{Customer\ Acquisition\ Cost}$$

Customer Retention Cost (CRC)—The CRC is the CAC equivalent for managing customer retention and engagement. Customer Success organizations and strategies vary widely from one company to another and this makes precise measurements difficult. Plus, there are not commonly available benchmarks for CRC. Still, you should attempt to incorporate CRC into your financial reporting if the precision validates the cost of measuring it. Costs that should be included in CRC are Customer Success Team salaries and wages, benefits and taxes, stock-based comp, and allocations for overhead and facility expenses; Post-Contract Support activities designed to improve ongoing customer engagement such as on-site training and end user marketing (blog posts, email campaigns, webinars) as well as any software required to support these activities; salaries and wages for any employees who engage customers directly for issue resolution should be included.

Customer Satisfaction (CSAT) Score—The CSAT Score differs from NPS in that CSAT measures customer satisfaction with the company's service, whereas NPS measures customer loyalty. Additionally, CSAT questionnaires use service-specific questions that focus on aspects of the customer's experience, e.g., "How would you rate the user interface?" and typically include multiple questions.

Customer Success Attach Rate (CSAR)—The CSAR measures the Post-Contract Support, or PCS, Bookings associated with a specific contract.

D

Daily Active Users to Monthly Active Users (DAU/MAU)—The DAU/MAU ratio is a measure of customer engagement. A high DAU/MAU ratio among end users implies that customers use your app frequently. The inverse is true for a low ratio.

Deferred Revenue—Deferred Revenue, also called Unearned Revenue, is a balance sheet account that represents the liability associated with the delivery of a SaaS product as required by contract. For an individual contract, Deferred Revenue is equal to all of the revenue expected to be recognized over the period as defined by the invoice. Enterprise SaaS companies typically require up-front annual payment for new or renewal contracts. On the date an invoice is issued, the SaaS company records the value of the invoice as Deferred Revenue and books the same amount to Accounts Receivable: debit Accounts Receivable and credit Deferred Revenue. When the customer pays the invoice amount, the company credits Accounts Receivable and debits Cash. Receipt of payment does not affect Deferred Revenue. Assuming that the invoice is for an annual term, the company records revenue in each month the revenue is earned. Therefore, the company will debit Deferred Revenue by one-twelfth of the invoice amount and credit Subscription Revenue by the same amount. On the Balance Sheet, Deferred Revenue is divided into Short-Term and Long-Term accounts. Short-Term Deferred Revenue is that which will be recognized within the next twelve months. Long-Term Deferred Revenue is that amount of revenue expected to be recognized after the next twelve months. For example, a $360,000 TCV deal with a three-year term and paid up front will generate $120,000 in Short-Term Deferred Revenue and $240,000 in Long-Term Deferred Revenue at date of invoicing. Each month, the company will credit Short-Term Deferred Revenue by $10,000 and debit Subscription Revenue by $10,000. On the one-year anniversary of the invoice date, the company will move the second year of Deferred Revenue into Short-Term Deferred Revenue and continue the monthly revenue recognition cadence for Subscription Revenue.

E

Escalation Rate—The Escalation Rate is a Customer Success metric that measures the percentage of customer inquiries that require follow-up support such as researching a customer-reported product issue. Although the Escalation Rate is just the opposite of the FCR, it's nonetheless important to track because the specific drivers can provide insight into the customer use cases and identify product functionality that needs to be incorporated into the product roadmap.

F

First Contact Resolution Rate (FCR)—The FCR represents the percentage of customer support calls that are resolved in the initial call. You can use this metric to get insight into customer engagement and satisfaction, product functionality, and skill level of the customer support team because the FCR is a function of all of these factors. The challenge is to identify the specific drivers of the FCR.

First Response Time—Customer support response time is a leading indicator of customer satisfaction. It is a function of customer support staffing and training.

Free Cash Flow (FCF)—The sum of cash flow from operations and the use of cash for investing activities. This is the most appropriate measure of a company's burn rate because it includes all expenses related to operating the business irrespective of the financing model. Cash flow from financing activities is not relevant because companies make different choices on funding strategy, specifically relating to the mix of equity and debt, based on market conditions that are unrelated to business operations. It is the best way in which to ensure benchmarks apply. FCF should be used in the RO40 growth metric.

G

Growth Efficiency or Growth Efficiency Index (GEI)—The Growth Efficiency or GEI metric is another rule of thumb. In my experience, I find application of this method somewhat useful for private SaaS companies but only as another parameter to augment your growth analysis. The main use case is in estimating burn rate at any given growth rate. The main shortcoming is lack of consensus on the standard, although blog posts suggest a figure of 1.0. Also, we can use a variety of other methods to benchmark your company's burn rate.

The equation is as follows:

$$Growth\ Efficiency = \frac{-1 * Free\ Cash\ Flow}{Net\ New\ ARR}$$

We can use the T2D3 rule to frame a hypothetical example. Let's assume that a company grows 3x annually from $6 million ARR to $18 million ARR resulting in $12 million of Net New ARR. The GEI suggests that you can burn $1 million per month to achieve this growth.

H

Human Capital Efficiency (HCE)—The single largest resource cost in a SaaS business model is people, i.e., payroll and related items. A proxy for operating efficiency is the ratio of Top-Line metrics, such as ARR or CARR and Revenue, to the number of employees. You can use any number of benchmark services such as the KeyBanc SaaS Survey or the OPEXEngine SaaS benchmarking service for comparison. Keep in mind that the HCE varies proportionally to size—the larger the company, the greater the scale—and does so more than other unit economic metrics.

I

Ideal Customer Profile (ICP)—An ICP, also referred to as the buyer persona, is a hypothetical description of the type of company that would most value the SaaS company's software.

M

Magic Number—A SaaS metric used to measure a company's sales efficiency using a ratio of New Subscription Revenue to Sales and Marketing expenses. Put another way, the Magic Number shows how much it costs to acquire $1 of subscription revenue. Any ratio above 1.0x means that your company generates more New Subscription Bookings than it spends to acquire the customer.

$$Magic\ Number = \frac{ARR_{period\ 1} - ARR_{period\ 0}}{Sales\ and\ Marketing\ Expense_{period\ 0}}$$

The most common formula is a ratio of the increase in ARR in the current period to the Sales and Marketing expenses in the prior period. The difference between the two periods should correspond to the length of the sales cycle. This is especially true for high growth, i.e., 3x annual ARR growth, companies. Investors' expectations are that the Magic Number should fall within a narrow range around 1.0x with any ratio above 3.0x indicating a phenomenal operational leverage. The Magic Number can be used for evaluating public companies with some adjustments. Public companies often do not publish their annual bookings numbers. Nor do they disclose the ARR at the end of the year, i.e., the Exit ARR. There are two ways in which to apply the Magic Number calculation if you do not have these two figures. Using year-over-year change in ARR, calculated using the Subscription Revenue in the fiscal fourth quarter and multiplying by four, will give a good proxy. As a reminder, the final quarter's numbers will be found in the 10-K for that year, although you may need to subtract the first three quarters from the annual numbers to get to fiscal quarter subscription revenue. The second approach is even simpler. You take the year-over-year change in Subscription Revenue and divide it into the Sales and Marketing expenses for the prior year. Be sure to note the method used.

The Magic Number often does not work well for Enterprise SaaS companies. High variation in the length of the sales cycle as measured by Average Days to Close makes defining the prior period Sales and Marketing expenses difficult. Therefore, in such cases, we use the same period for comparison. The resulting metric is often referred to as Sales Efficiency.

Marketing Channels

> **Affiliate Marketing**—This channel makes use of partners referred to as Distribution Partners or Affiliate Partners that manage a network of websites. SaaS companies will give the partner a specific link to post on their sites. Affiliates are paid for lead generation.

Content Marketing—Content Marketing refers to the creation of proprietary content for social media posts, company-hosted blogs, v-blogs, podcasts and webinars, articles, white papers, and any other material that will capture and maintain the attention of consumers, both before and after the sale.

Digital Advertising—Digital Advertising is the practice of purchasing space on websites to run static or video advertising.

Digital Marketing—Digital Marketing is a broad term because it refers to all online channels used to access potential consumers. It forms an essential part of the GTM strategy. We can subcategorize Digital Marketing into several groups.

Direct Notification—This term refers to email, mobile numbers (SMS/text), and push notifications used to acquire potential subscribers and maintain engagement with current customers.

Influencer Marketing—Influencers are individuals who have established a credibility among a specific demographic and who can wield this credibility to drive purchase decisions.

Search Engine Optimization (SEO)—SEO refers to the optimization of your company's website for maximum visibility to search engine algorithms.

Search Engine Marketing (SEM)—Search Engine Marketing refers to the use of paid advertisements that appear on search engine result pages.

Social Media Marketing—This channel involves establishing a presence on social media and engaging with both prospective and current customers.

Marketing-Qualified Lead (MQLs)—A customer lead generated by a marketing campaign and determined to be a potential customer based on a propensity or intent to purchase. This qualification is based on the lead's engagement with your brand and is often measured in response to inbound and outbound efforts, webinar attendance, online activities, and other engagement with the business's content.

N

Net Promoter Score (NPS)—The NPS is a customer satisfaction metric that measures a customer's likelihood of recommending a company's product or service.

New Feature Adoption—The New Feature Adoption can be measured as the median time it takes for all, or some target level, of the product's users to adopt the feature and the percentage of users who utilize the new feature.

Number of Events per Day per User—In this context, the word "event" refers to any activity undertaken by the user. For an Enterprise SaaS marketing technology company, an event may be the running of a specific marketing campaign. For an

SMM SaaS project management software company, an event may be the publishing of a project management instance. For a B2C SaaS survey company, an event may be the distribution of an individual survey.

Number of Sessions per Day per User—This Customer Success metric is typically defined as the number of logins per day.

O

On-Target Earnings (OTE)—OTE is the amount of an AE's annual compensation earned by achieving 100% of quota. At OTE, 50% of the AE's total compensation comes from salary and 50% from sales commission. For example, an AE with a base salary of $300,000 should have an annual quota set at a level where earning 100% of the quota will result in total annual compensation of $600,000.

Operating Expense Margins—Operating Expense Margins are the metrics calculated by dividing the Research and Development, Sales and Marketing, and, General and Administrative expenses into Total Revenue.

Operating Expense Ratios—Operating Expense Ratios refer to a set of metrics calculated by dividing Research and Development and General and Administrative expenses into Sales and Marketing. These metrics provide additional insight into the investments in these areas when compared to those of comparable companies.

P

Partnerships, Types of

Affiliate Program—This program involves a fee for referral arrangement with third parties that are in contact with the target customers.

Co-Marketing Program—In a Co-Marketing Program, a company works with another player in the same space and with similar target customers by collaborating on marketing events and content creation.

Co-Selling Partnership—In Co-Selling Partnerships, two companies with distinct software products agree to collaborate on their GTM strategies in targeting the same customers.

Reselling Partnerships—A Reselling Partnership involves a partner who distributes the product on behalf of the SaaS company.

Point Solution—A Point Solution refers to a SaaS product that addresses or supports a single functionality. A product that allows accounting teams to manage sales tax would be a Point Solution.

Professional Services Attach Rate (PSAR)—The PSAR measures the Professional Services Bookings Value divided by Total Subscription Software Bookings.

Q

Quick Ratio for SaaS—The term "Quick Ratio" is a finance concept that provides a simplistic metric for reporting a company's liquidity and is defined as Liquid Assets divided by Current Liabilities. Any number greater than 1.0 is good. In SaaS parlance, the Quick Ratio is a good metric in that it's simple and uses 1.0 as a benchmark. It differs in that the QR is a growth metric calculated as the dollar growth in recurring revenue divided by the loss of recurring revenue. The specific calculation is as follows:

$$SaaS\ Quick\ Ratio\ =\ \frac{New\ and\ Expansion\ Recurring\ Revenue}{Contraction\ and\ Churn\ of\ Recurring\ Revenue}$$

Where recurring revenue can be either Annual or Monthly.

R

Remaining Performance Obligation (RPO)—A company's RPO represents the total future performance obligations arising from contractual relationships. More specifically, RPO is the sum of the invoiced amount and the future amounts not yet invoiced for a contract with a customer. The former amount resides on the balance sheet as Deferred Revenue and has always been reported as required by GAAP. The latter obligation, also referred to as Backlog, makes up the non-invoiced amount of the Total Contract Value metric. Thus, RPO equals the sum of Deferred Revenue and Backlog.

Retention Rates

DBNER/DBNR—These acronyms stand for Dollar-Based Net Expansion Rate and Dollar-Based Net Retention, which are used interchangeably.

Expansion Rate—The additional recurring revenue generated from existing customers through either Upsells or Cross-Sells, expressed as a percentage of existing ARR. Enterprise SaaS companies use this metric because the ACV of new customers can be expanded by capturing a larger share of their technology budgets either by selling to more users or by selling more software products to the customer.

Gross Churn Rate—The percentage of ARR that does not renew at the contract's renewal date. For an Enterprise SaaS company, we express this metric in dollars and not customer count because the revenue impact is more closely related to change in absolute dollar churn. Hence, we refer to this as Gross Dollar Churn Rate. SMM and B2C SaaS companies use customer count, and we simply call this Gross Churn Rate.

Net Churn Rate/Net Expansion Rate—The net result of Gross Churn Rate and the Expansion Rate. Note that Net Churn Rate is shown as a negative number and Net Expansion Rate as a positive number.

Renewal Rate—The existing ARR or customers that we successfully renew on the renewal date as a percentage of the total up for renewal. This metric is more common to Enterprise SaaS and SMM SaaS companies because a large portion of the customer base is under contract, typically annual, and therefore not eligible to churn until the contract renewal date. B2C SaaS companies rely on month-to-month contracts, so the Renewal and Retention Rates will be the same.

Retention Rate—Retention Rate is expressed either as a dollar-based metric or customer count-based metric. Enterprise and SMM SaaS companies use dollar-based retention because of the large variance in the customer ACV. So the loss of one customer may or may not have a material impact on ARR. Contraction in one customer contract would impact ARR, but a count-based metric would not account for this change. Finally, these customers tend to be more stable and less likely to churn. Alternatively, B2C SaaS companies use a count-based metric because average ACV among the customer base is more similar and the customers are more likely to churn.

Retention Rate versus Renewal Rate—Note the difference between Renewal Rate and Retention Rate. The Renewal Rate will always be lower than the Retention Rate because the denominator of the former is smaller than that of the latter. As an example, consider a company with $250,000 of Exposed ARR in a specific quarter and this makes up 25% of its $1 million ARR base. The company renews 80% or $200,000 of this Exposed AR. The retention rate during this quarter is 95% or $950,000 of its $1 million ARR base. The $950,000 numerator is the sum of the Renewed ARR, $200,000, and the ARR that was not up for renewal, $750,000.

Revenue Recognition Date—The date on which the company has met all revenue recognition requirements per GAAP/IFRS as determined by the CFO. This is a change driven by the adoption of ASC 606, which created a new revenue recognition criterion by merging the GAAP and IFRS concepts. Under ASC 606, revenue is recognized when the following criteria are met: (1) customer contract exists with (2) identifiable performance obligations (3) transaction price determined and (4) allocated appropriately; and (5) satisfaction of the performance obligation.

Rule of Forty (RO40)—The RO40 postulates that a SaaS company's combined growth rate and profitability should exceed 40%. Companies can achieve this benchmark through high growth and negative profitability or the inverse with low growth and high profitablity. Either approach leads to outsized enterprise values compared to peers with lower RO40 values. The RO40 serves as a yardstick that allows SaaS companies with a wide variety of GTM strategies to benchmark their growth. For the calculation, the growth rate is best measured using the year-over-year comparison of ARR, although Subscription Bookings is a valid approach. Profitability is best measured using the FCF definition, which is the sum of the company's cash flow from operations and cash flow used for investing, typically capital expenditures.

S

Sales-Accepted Leads (SALs)—Marketing-qualified leads that indicate a high propensity or intent to purchase and are submitted for sales review and acceptance. Once the sales team has accepted these leads, Sales Development Representatives (SDRs) will contact the lead to confirm marketing's assessment of the lead and to determine the degree to which the prospective customer fits with the Ideal Customer Profile. The SDR will also begin identifying the prospective customer's employees who are most important to the purchase decision.

Sales Capacity Plan—The Sales Capacity Plan provides a forecast of expected annual production. The output is a function of (1) number of quota-carrying sales representatives, i.e., AEs, (2) their Quota expressed in ACV for both subscription and non-recurring revenue such as professional services, and (3) their Productivity, expressed as a percentage of total expected annual production. The Productivity factor is used to account for lower-than-expected Bookings based on internal and external factors. The inverse of this term is called the Over-Assignment Factor.

Sales Commission Rate—The percentage of the Bookings value earned by an individual Sales Representative for closing an opportunity. The following two components are involved in calculating the Direct Sales Commission rate: (1) **Base Commission Rate (BCR)**—This is the sales commission rate earned by a Sales Representative for closing Bookings contracts and is calculated as a percentage of the Bookings value and (2) **Accelerator**—The Accelerator is an additional percentage added to the BCR for all Bookings above a certain amount, which is usually the Sales Representative's quota.

Sales Commission Rate, Fully Loaded—The percentage of the ACV earned by the individual Sales Representative as well as all qualified team members for closing an opportunity. Other members of the sales team typically include sales management, sales operations, and sales engineers. Companies with a sales partner (Partnership, OEM, Channel) strategy will incentivize the appropriate team to avoid conflicts between direct and partner channels.

Sales Efficiency—An adaptation of the Magic Number for Enterprise SaaS companies. Long sales cycles and the variance in time of the sales cycles make defining the "prior period" Sales and Marketing expenses difficult. Therefore, in such cases, we use the Sales and Marketing expenses in the same period as the New Subscription Bookings, whether actual or forecasted. For example, if you project $20 million in New Subscription Bookings for a given fiscal year, then your Sales and Marketing expenses should, in theory, be ~$20 million to achieve a 1.0x ratio. Keep in mind the fact that ratios calculated in this manner will be lower than a Magic Number calculation exactly because you are using current-period Sales and Marketing expenses.

$$Sales\ Efficiency = \frac{New\ Subscription\ Bookings\ _{period\ 0}}{Annual\ Sales\ and\ Marketing\ Expense\ _{period\ 0}}$$

Sales Opportunity—An opportunity is a prospective customer at an advanced stage in the sales process with probability of closing that can be reasonably estimated. A typical set of opportunity stages looks like this: Prospecting (5%–10%), Investigation/In Discussion (15%–30%), Proposal Price Quote (40%–60%), Negotiation/Review (80%), Closed Won (100%); Closed Lost (0%).

Sales Pipeline—The Sales Pipeline is the value of all current opportunities. This metric is often shown as unweighted, meaning the dollar value of the deal, and as weighted, meaning the probability-weighted value of your opportunities.

Sales Pipeline Coverage—This is the ratio of Required Bookings over the Target Bookings, with the latter defined by the Operating Plan (or Budget). A general rule of thumb for the Sales Pipeline Coverage metric is 4.0x. This means that a company should have four times as much ACV in its pipeline as its Target Bookings. This is a period-specific ratio, meaning that the timing of the pipeline coverage ACV is measured against the period in which the opportunities are expected to close.

Sales-Qualified Lead (SQL)—A Sales Opportunity that the SDR has confirmed to fit the Ideal Customer Profile deemed ready for the next step in the sales process. The SDR will record the lead as an SQL and introduce the lead to the AE. The actual introduction is typically a live call or video meeting between the AE and the primary contact(s) at the prospective customer. The date of the call or meeting is the point at which the SAL should be considered an SQL for reporting purposes.

Sales Representative Productivity—We use a variety of metrics to measure productivity, but the most common are the following:

- **Quota Achievement**—Percentage of quota attained for a given time period in aggregate for all sales representatives and by individual sales representatives.

- **Participation Rate**—Percentage of sales representatives that achieve quota in a given time period.

- **Win Rate by Sales Representative**—Closed/Won Opportunities divided by All Opportunities as defined above for an individual sales representative.

- **Sales Ramp**—Time to reach high quota attainment, typically defined as consistent Quota Achievement above estimated team productivity as defined in the sales capacity planning model.

- **Sales Representative Staffing**—Recruiting/attrition (regrettable and non-regrettable).

Sales Representatives, Types of

Account Executive (AE)—The AE is the key customer-facing member of the Direct Sales team responsible for closing deals to create new customers. Enterprise SaaS companies build complex products and sell into large corporations.

Business Development Representative (BDR)—In larger organizations, the SDR job transitions into separate roles that manage inbound and outbound activities. The SDR will focus exclusively on qualifying inbound leads in support of the AEs. The BDR assumes the role of outbound activities, leverage emails, phone calls, and social selling tools to add Sales Opportunities in the pipeline.

Inside Sales Representative (ISR)—An ISR manages inbound customer leads generated by marketing campaigns.

Sales Development Representative (SDR)—SDRs support AEs by prospecting for Sales Opportunities and engaging with the lead to generate interest in a sale. When the potential customer is deemed to have high propensity to purchase the software, the SDR notifies an AE who will work to convert the lead into a sale.

Sales Engineer (SE)—SEs support the AEs by facilitating sales opportunity discussions with deep technical expertise on the product.

Sales Velocity—The Sales Velocity metric shows how much revenue you are adding per day over the length of the sales cycle. It is calculated as the product of the number of closed opportunities, the average subscription ACV of these opportunities, and the Win Rate with the result divided by the Sales Cycle.

$$\text{Sales Velocity} = \frac{\text{No. of Sales Opps x ACV x Win Rate}}{\text{Sales Cycle}}$$

Serviceable Available Market (SAM)—The segment of the TAM targeted by your service which is within your geographical reach. The SAM gives you a much better sense of how much revenue you can realistically bring in with your product, but the TAM is useful in indicating how much room there is for potential growth.

Serviceable Obtainable Market (SOM)—The portion of SAM that you can realistically capture. The SOM is typically defined by the market share for your specific service versus all other competitors with a comparable offering.

Subscription Revenue Gross Margin—The gross profit margin of the subscription software revenue only. Gross Margin is the percentage of revenue remaining after subtracting the direct costs associated with the delivery of the hosted SaaS product in the period the revenues are generated. These direct costs fall into seven categories: Hosting and Infrastructure, Customer Support, Professional Services, Cloud Operations/Platform Support, Capitalized Internal-Use Software and Purchased Technology, Third-Party Fees, and Overhead Allocations.

T

T2D3—T2D3 is a rule of thumb that defines best-in-class revenue growth. It postulates that from revenue in single-digit millions, revenue growth should triple for the first two years, then double for the subsequent three years. For example, a company that reaches $2 million in revenue in year zero should grow to $6 million in year one, $18 million in year two, $36 million in year three, $72 million in year four, and $144 million in year five. This rule of thumb is based on growth trajectories achieved by the highest growth technology companies over the past two decades.

Total Addressable Market (TAM)—The gross dollar value available for purchasing your SaaS product. For your company, it will refer to the total revenue you can generate in selling your offering. For fundraising, you will need to conduct a TAM Analysis, which should provide a detailed estimate of the market you intend to serve. Remember that the TAM will grow over time. You should incorporate these growth expectations into your strategic thinking.

Time Spent on the Product per Day and per Session on a Per-User Basis—This Customer Success metric is often a good measure of end user engagement. One word of caution, though: the time spent in the product may not equate to value added. If your application simply allowed a company to move a function online but has not made users significantly more efficient, then you are not adding value. So do not be fooled by a high time spent on the product metric.

Time to Live (TTL)—Time it takes to complete implementation and get customers live on the product.

Time to Grow (TTG)—A Professional Services metric that measures the time it takes to expand the ACV of the customer via upselling and/or cross-selling.

Time to Value (TTV)—A Professional Services metric that measures the time it takes to get the customer to realize the full extent of value from the product.

W

Win Rate—The ratio of Opportunities Won over the total opportunities in the sales pipeline.

$$\text{Win Rate} = \frac{\text{Won Opportunities}}{\text{Won Opportunities} + \text{Lost Opportunities}}$$

U

Unit Economics—The term "Unit Economics" refers to the measurement of the revenues and costs associated with an individual customer. It's the atomic-level view of the business in that this unit cannot be subdivided. SaaS companies use an average of several customers as the unit, often grouping customers into cohorts or segments. Viewing the company's performance in this way will allow you to gain an understanding of profitability on a per-customer basis and measure your performance with established benchmarks.

User Retention by Time Period—B2C SaaS companies that operate in spaces with low barriers to entry, low switching costs, and a high number of substitutes closely track the performance of monthly cohorts with cohort defined as the number of customers acquired in a given month. Such consumers can be fickle and may churn out quickly. Therefore, you must monitor the slope of the retention curve over the subsequent month. One way to report on this curve is to use a set of metrics defined by the percentage of users active as time progresses. For example, the metric D30 refers to the percentage of active users who were acquired in the prior month, i.e., Month Zero, on the thirtieth day of the following month, i.e., Month One. You will see every variety of this metric: D7, D15, D30, D60 in days; W1, W2, W3, etc. in weeks; and M1, M2, M3, etc. in months.

Printed in the USA
CPSIA information can be obtained
at www.ICGtesting.com
LVHW092004260823
756254LV00011B/260/J